SE FORM

Date March 10-46

t that the pictures taken of me by

proofs of which are hereto

Jasgur for the purpose of illus-

manner.   I hereby certify and

rs of age.

_____
MODEL

achrome — Outdoor

First published in Great Britain in 1991 by
Sidgwick & Jackson Limited

Designed by Rick Sullivan

ISBN 0-283-99852-0

Typeset by Spectrum Typesetting Ltd, London E2
Printed in the United Kingdom by Butler and Tanner Ltd
Frome and London
for Sidgwick & Jackson Limited
18-21 Cavaye Place
London SW10 9PG

THE BIRTH OF
MARILYN

THE LOST PHOTOGRAPHS OF
NORMA JEAN BY JOSEPH JASGUR

JEANNIE SAKOL

Sidgwick & Jackson
London

A day at Zuma Beach. A step towards stardom…

'God helps those who invent what they need.'

Lillian Hellman

Contents

STEPS TO STARDOM

'My arrival in school, with painted lips and darkened brows, started everyone buzzing. Why I was a siren, I hadn't the faintest idea. I didn't want to be kissed, and I didn't dream of being seduced by a duke or a movie star. The truth was that with all my lipstick and mascara and precocious curves, I was as unresponsive as a fossil. But I seemed to affect people quite otherwise.'

Marilyn Monroe

'...This girl – her name was Norma Jean Dougherty – came in and asked if I thought she could be a model ... *Could she*!'

Paul Parry

She hated wearing underwear. She loved taking her clothes off and being photographed naked. She wanted more than anything to be famous and to be loved. She used men like paper hankies, tucking some into her bosom for emergency purposes, tossing others away without so much as a sigh or backward glance.

Men, of course, had always used and abused her from motives ranging from transient slam-bam lust to the sadistic contempt that men of power confuse with pleasure when they tantalize helpless women with hopes of hopeless dreams come true.

Yet, throughout her life, there proved to be one constant, one adoring and enduring lover: the camera. While men's eyes saw a succulent peach ripe for the plucking, the camera's eye consistently found much more. In the early days, it discovered a startling and unsettling fusion of sweetness, vulnerability and a volcanic sexual daring waiting to be uncorked. Men's eyes saw the surface. The camera's eye exposed the fears, anxiety and gut courage behind her mask of seductive availability.

Men might be demanding, resentful, cranky, spiteful – driven by emotions they didn't understand; men might turn cruel and nasty. But the camera? Never. The camera adored her regardless. The camera was the all-adoring mother she never had, the father she never knew, the comforting friends and suitors who never deserted her no matter what she did, and always left her feeling beautiful, satisfied and beloved.

From her earliest copulation with the camera, what came through was her urgent, pleading message: *'Love me. Make me famous.'* The camera did love her. The camera licked her skin and caressed her hair. To the camera, her eyes conveyed a subtle mix of shyness and carnality. There was the promise of unmentionable delight in her glossy full-blown lips. Even in the early girl-next-door cheesecake days, the camera somehow set her apart from the others and found grace in her awkwardness – and primitive innocence in her assumed sophistication.

Like the future Princess Diana, Norma Jean Dougherty was eighteen when the camera first fell in love with her. Unlike Lady Diana and her privileged Barbara Cartland background, Norma Jean was American Dickens from the start. Born illegitimate in a Los Angeles charity ward, she never knew her father and, in fact, his actual identity remains clouded. Her mother suffered mental breakdowns and was institutionalized. Foster families abused the little girl emotionally and sexually. For a while, she lived in an orphanage across the street from RKO Studios. At fifteen, she dropped out of school. A year later, she married James Dougherty and moved into a one-room apartment with a bed that pulled down from a cupboard.

By then, it was June 1942. America was at war. Jim joined the Merchant Marines and took his teen wife with him to his training base on Catalina Island where her skimpy sunsuits evoked wolf calls that fuelled and fed her insatiable appetite for approval. When her husband's unit was shipped out, she went to work at a defence plant where the first professional camera found her and set her on the rocky road to fame and misfortune.

Army photographer David Conover's assignment was to shoot pretty young women 'doing their part' for the war effort. His photographs in *Yank* and *Stars and Stripes* confirmed her secret fantasy. The orphan who had fallen asleep each night watching the RKO Studio sign was now convinced she, too, could be a movie star like Betty Grable, Rita Hayworth, Lana Turner and Ava Gardner. All she needed was to reach that first step on the ladder.

The Photographs that Spawn a Friendship... and a New Life

'Girls ask me all the time how they can be like Marilyn Monroe, and I tell them, if they had one-tenth of the hard work and gumption that that girl had, they'd be on their way.'

Emmeline Snively

Nineteen forty-six was a watershed year for the world as well as for Norma Jean Dougherty. The war was over. Euphoria swept over America in spasms of hope and expectation. Peace — it was going to be wonderful. Anything was possible. For Norma Jean, the days of ration cards, leg make-up and West Coast fears of Japanese bombs were over. More than 291,000 American men had died and the rest were coming home to resume their lives.

Norma Jean was glad for her husband's sake that he had survived; she wished him no ill. But her post-war dream did not include him. She didn't want to be a wife. She wanted something more glamorous and exciting. Other American women might be singing, 'I Don't Want to Walk Without You' to their returning lovers and husbands, but not Norma Jean. If she was to become a model or a movie star, she'd have to walk alone.

For Norma Jean, 1946 was to be the first year of her new life — the year Marilyn Monroe was born. While post-war euphoria galvanized America with an atmosphere of high expectations and glowing possibilities, Norma Jean asked for a divorce, moved into the Studio Club where young hopefuls stayed, and signed up with Emmeline Snively's Hollywood Blue Book Model Agency. She was ready to have it all.

On 6 March 1946, Hollywood photographer Joseph Jasgur was processing some celebrity shots taken the previous night at the famed Trocadero. Night clubs and other celebrity events were his regular beat for the *Hollywood Citizen-News* and various movie magazines. An insatiable public hungered for informal candid shots of their favourite stars: Humphrey Bogart and Lauren Bacall, Bette Davis, Joan Crawford, Gary Cooper, Lana Turner, Mickey Rooney, Ava Gardner — the instantly recognizable stars, yes, and also the newcomers, the cheesecake starlets and beefcake boys on their way to the top.

When the telephone rang, he was wearing his protective rubber apron and making eight-by-ten prints with his enlarger. This was before the invention of the answering machine, and with both hands busy, he was tempted to ignore the phone — whoever it was would call back. But whoever it was wanted him now and refused to hang up.

An exasperated Joseph Jasgur answered abruptly, but softened when he learned it was his dear friend, Emmeline Snively, director of the Hollywood Blue Book Model Agency. A dignified, motherly woman known for wearing hats and gloves in a town of rampant informality, Emmeline was widely respected for the strict rules of comportment she demanded from her 'girls'.

Could Joe do her a favour?

'Another newcomer?'

Another newcomer.

'With great potential?'

'I don't know.'

'And no money?'

'No, Joe.'

Nearly half a century later, Jasgur sighs as he relishes the memory. 'And you want me to do some

'She was not glamorous; she was not even pretty, but her appeal was genuine, a child's appeal – sweet and disarming.'

Walter Bernstein

test shots, Emmeline?'

'Just a few. To see if the camera likes her . . . if it isn't an imposition.'

Far from being an imposition, taking test shots for Emmeline was Joe's way of returning her many favours to him, including tips on magazine assignments. The late Forties were peaches and cream days, innocent days before *Playboy* and *Hustler* when the ideal was the fresh-faced girl next door looking provocative but nice. The captivated man was theoretically tempted to take her home to mother – not to bed.

'What's her name?'

Norma Jean Dougherty: nineteen years old; height five feet, six inches; weight one hundred and eighteen pounds; bust, thirty-six; waist, twenty-four; hips, thirty-four; eyes blue; hair brown and much too curly.

'Send her over.'

The young hopeful was there almost before he hung up. He was still wearing his rubberized darkroom apron and had still not finished cropping and printing the blow-up in his enlarger.

She stood framed in the doorway of his studio, the bright California sunshine behind her, her features obscured in shadow. All he could see of her was her paper-doll outline in silhouette against a distant wall.

'Mr Jasgur?' Her voice was breathless, whispery, as if she'd run for a bus and missed it. What millions would later adore and try to imitate, Jasgur attributed to nerves. He tried to put her at ease.

'Come in,' he said kindly.

She had rehearsed her little speech: 'Mrs Snively said I should come over and see you and you would take some test shots . . . ' Here she paused and swallowed hard; so much depended on what came next, ' . . . and tell her what you think.'

'Now let me take a look at you and see what I can do,' he told his visitor.

What he saw was not too encouraging. Her hips were too broad and would photograph even broader if he didn't take special pains. Her loose pink wool sweater and checked pedal-pushers only exaggerated the imperfections of her figure and emphasized her need to lose some weight. As for her hair, it was thick and wild and reddish brown, its natural curliness obviously impossible to control – although she had equally obviously tried to do just that with a saucy beret. The colour, Jasgur realized, was totally wrong for her blue eyes and peach blossom skin tones. If ever a girl should be blonde it was this girl who was so patiently enduring his professional scrutiny.

She seemed to him yet one more starry-eyed youngster, one of the vast army of girls destined by fate and poverty to work in factories or as waitresses, whose only hope for a better life was through their looks. His heart went out to her as it had to many before her.

She didn't have a chance, he thought, until he looked into her eyes. Her face was pretty enough in a wholesome kind of way. Her nose was a bit too broad but he knew he could make it look thinner through clever placement of his camera. He could also compensate for the slight weakness in her chin and make her appear taller by shooting from low angles. Her mouth was lush and full, he was relieved to note. Getting back to her eyes, he realized that here was something different.

He had never quite got used to the eyes of young hopefuls. However poised and confident they might appear, their eyes were always a giveaway, a fusion of fear and pleading, a terrible urgency, an SOS of the soul, begging for help and offering anything that might be demanded to get it. Norma Jean's eyes were none of the above. A lovely vivid blue, they gazed at him with a calm and quiet dignity, neither arrogant nor seductive. There was *something* there. Reflecting on that moment, Jasgur shakes his head with an amazement that has never left him in forty-five years. 'I never thought that *something* would take her so far.'

It being a busy day for Joe, his first impulse was to ask Norma Jean to come back the following day. But something, perhaps the something in her eyes, persuaded him to change his mind. The California sun was shining in the alley outside his studio door. He could spare ten, maybe fifteen minutes, to make a few test shots and at the same time meet his long-standing obligation to Emmeline.

While Norma Jean ran a comb through her unruly hair, managing to tame it somewhat, Jasgur loaded his $2\frac{1}{4} \times 2\frac{1}{4}$ Rolleiflex, the camera he preferred to the then popular speed graphic. 'The Rolleiflex gave me a large square negative, much better for cropping to any configuration. I believe in getting good negatives. With the Rollei, you look down into the camera and you see precisely the picture you're getting. You have to wind it up for every shot — clumsy, sure, but you get good images,' says Jasgur.

He still has the Rolleiflex camera he used to shoot Norma Jean's test shots. It's among his sizable collection of cameras dating back to his early days as a photo-journalist in Detroit in the Thirties. The 'Norma Jean' Rollei is among his favourites; he still uses it today.

If you look carefully at Jasgur's first Norma Jean session, you'll see in the background a wall with bars on the windows. Joe drove me over to see it. In a milieu where the sight of a vintage Rolls, Lamborghini or London taxi causes nary a stir, his ramshackle 1973 Plymouth Satellite prompts good-natured smiles and scattered applause.

If you'd like to see the historic wall for yourself, it's in a mews-like alley behind Beverly Boulevard, alongside Poinsettia Place in West Hollywood and easy to find on an ordinary Los Angeles street map. Locals know of the wall's significance and often picnic beside it in the quiet alley. There is no plaque or any other indication of its Marilyn Monroe link.

Near the corner of Poinsettia and Beverly where the El Coyote Restaurant now stands, there was a little coffee-shop type of restaurant, Joe recalled. 'That's where we went after the first session. Norma Jean was hungry. We had hamburgers and Cokes and French fries,' he recited, savouring each item as if it were Beluga and bubbly.

The fifteen minutes he had 'stolen' from his schedule had lengthened to over an hour. An instant rapport developed between him and the unschooled neophyte. 'It wasn't sexual. It was a kind of mutual respect — she for me as a photographer, me for her as a person. She was amazingly private and self-contained. She didn't giggle or chatter on and on the way others did.

'More than any woman I've ever met before or since, she was totally comfortable in front of the camera. She was relaxed, no trace of self-consciousness. Even in those formative days, I think she trusted the camera more than she trusted people.' Having said that, Jasgur added, 'She probably trusted me more than anyone at that time. And I never took advantage of that trust.'

This principled behaviour was tested almost at once. Following the first session, Jasgur asked her if she had ever been in a darkroom, or seen photographs developed and printed. At that time, there was a hoary old photographers' joke about 'developing a friendship in the darkroom'. Photographers were notorious as a breed for luring pretty young things into the intimate red-lit sanctum where mysterious rituals were performed and fame and immortality awaited the emerging images created by the photographer wizard.

'She wasn't that busty and she had a little heavy hips. And she had freckles all over. And there were some little varicose veins in there. She was just like the girl next door.'

Lawrence Schiller

'She knew exactly what to do — her movements, her hands, her body were just perfect. She was the sexiest.'

Earl Moran

The rituals often escalated into the sexual, with the resultant grave misunderstanding on the part of the pretty young thing who would naïvely assume she had paid her dues and wonder why she wasn't famous.

In his own way, Joseph Jasgur was as romantic of nature as Norma Jean Dougherty. A young man's joy emerges from his weathered face. 'It was the first time she had ever been in a darkroom. She was as quiet as a schoolgirl, like she was in a museum or a church. The process fascinated her — the developing and printing.

'"Magic," she whispered, when her face slowly began to materialize on a blank sheet of paper. "*Magic!*"'

There was no need to whisper, he assured her. Try as she would to speak normally, her voice remained hushed. Nerves, he thought at first, or anxiety about the results. He quickly realized he was wrong. She did not react like the others who were 'thrilled to pieces' by the experience.

'Her purpose was to learn. She looked at her pictures dispassionately — as if they were of someone else. Her questions were shrewd and right to the point. What were her best angles? How could she minimize her hips? How could she improve her hair and her smile?

The results of the first hurried session proved to Joe what every photographer knows but sometimes forgets. The camera lens is mightier than the naked eye. Norma Jean was awkward but incredibly appealing. She had a presence that attracted attention and held it. The awkwardness would, he was sure, disappear with time and a little experience. The appeal would grow. Together, she and Joe examined the finished prints. There was silence in Jasgur's studio. He suddenly understood that she wanted to know what he would tell Emmeline Snively but that some inner reserve prevented her from asking him outright.

'I'm sorry I didn't have more time today,' he began.

She nodded as if barely hearing him, as if it didn't much matter to her one way or another.

'If you're free next week, I thought we might do a session up at Malibu. Zuma Beach, maybe.'

Again, the vague nod accompanied by a brief hint of a smile.

'I'll call Mrs Snively and let her know, OK Norma Jean?'

The smile exploded into a burst of gleeful radiance. She pulled her beret down as far as it would go over her wayward curls and spun herself across the studio like a wood nymph doing a series of pirouettes. A fleeting kiss on Joe's cheek and she was gone, Joe calling after her, 'Bring your bathing suit.'

Less than a week later, Joe took Norma Jean to the top of the Don Lee Towers above the 'Hollywood' sign overlooking the city. Norma Jean wore a plaid shirt and dungarees. Among Joe's props was a telescope whose major function was to give his subjects something to do with their hands. With Norma Jean, he thought of something more impish.

'Stick out your tongue!'

'Oh, Joe — I can't!' She pouted the way little girls protest about doing their homework.

He assumed a paternal posture. 'Yes, you can, Norma Jean.'

'No, I can't.' She stamped her foot in further little girl mockery.

'You trust me, don't you, Norma Jean?'

She hesitated before nodding her head yes.

Joe saw she was enjoying the naughty girl game. 'Then do what Joe asks you. Stick out your tongue!'

With a merry laugh, she complied with evident satisfaction.
'Good girl!'

'No one manufactured her astonishing joy of life, the sheer exuberance that caused her to squeal with unrestrained delight at even the simplest little pleasures.'

Ted Jordan

Moulding Innocence

Emmeline agreed with Joe on two counts: Norma Jean's hair needed to be lightened and straightened. And her smile needed some thinking about, too, though Joe didn't see anything wrong with it. Emmeline felt there was room for improvement but hadn't figured out what to do. Yet. Encouraged by the raw possibilities in Joe's first session, Emmeline concluded that Norma Jean was worth a small investment of time and money. As she said at the time, 'It is the aim and privilege of the Bluebook Model organization to help select, organize and promote newcomers on their way to careers in modelling and theatre and motion pictures.'

The agency's offices were in the Ambassador Hotel on Wilshire Boulevard, the film colony's first grand hotel which opened its palatial doors on New Year's Day 1921, and closed them in 1990 on orders from new owner Donald J. Trump. During its heyday in the Thirties and Forties, film stars, visiting royalty like the then Prince of Wales and the merely rich and fun-loving flocked to its exotic gardens, swimming pool, tennis courts and its world-famous Coconut Grove night club. In its waning years, tragedy struck in June 1968, with the murder of Senator Robert Kennedy, minutes after his triumphant speech of victory in the California primary.

In 1946, two of Hollywood's most celebrated hair stylists were Frank and Joseph. Their salon was across Wilshire Boulevard from the Ambassador Hotel. What's more they were close friends of Emmeline's and an integral part of the close-knit inner circle that included Joseph Jasgur. Frank and Joseph agreed that Norma Jean's hair desperately needed help. They bleached it lighter in stages, gave her a reverse permanent wave to straighten it enough to be manageable, and cut it just enough to give it shape without sacrificing the glamour of bouncing, wind-swept hair.

At first glance, Norma Jean's smile was fine. Yet Emmeline was besieged by a nagging doubt she could not define. Norma Jean patiently smiled and smiled under her mentor's piercing gaze until Emmeline was able to isolate the problem. It was the space between the top of her mouth and the end of the nose. The space was too short. There wasn't enough room for her upper lip.

The solution? 'Try smiling with your upper lip drawn down … a slight pouting look.'

It was a piece of advice that would change Norma Jean's appearance subtly but substantially; it would become part of Marilyn Monroe's persona for the rest of her life. To this day, Marilyn impersonators invariably mimic their heroine's mouth quivering slightly with the effort of lowering her smile. It was a mannerism that began as a solution to a problem and became a personal trademark.

A Day at Zuma Beach

Malibu today is known familiarly as the Colony, where film stars have paid millions for quite modest houses that create a formidable barricade between the Pacific Coast Highway and the wide white

'It was almost as if she had been waiting for a button to be pushed, and when it was ... a door opened and you saw a treasure of gold and jewels.'

Lee Strasberg

beach fronting the Pacific Ocean. It is a lyrically beautiful stretch of California coastline, a paradise for the barefoot. The salty air and sea breezes are gentle. Small sailboats frolic in the calm swells with little fear of the turbulence they would find in the Atlantic or the Gulf of Mexico.

In the spring of 1946, the beach at Malibu was as it is today, as God and nature made it, only more primitive in its surroundings. Pre-dating today's designer shacks was a scattering of authentic hovels inhabited by worshippers of the sun and sea who took whatever work they could get to support their modest and free-wheeling lifestyle.

Joseph Jasgur frequently chose Malibu as a location for shooting pin-up features on models and starlets. Magazines, newspapers and wire services couldn't seem to get enough of comely young women in two-piece bathing suits or sunsuits. A special section of Malibu that he had come to know and love was called Zuma Beach. For some unknown reason, the light and the atmosphere at Zuma seemed to be just that little bit better . . . he couldn't really explain why. It just was and it was where he brought Norma Jean, her two two-piece swimsuits and a back seat loaded down with cameras, lenses and props. Norma Jean lay back against the front seat of his 1942 Lincoln custom coupé, eyes closed, running her fingers through her auburn hair. Jasgur watched the sun beams dance across her relaxed features. Whatever her cares and anxieties, the sea air and the promise of adventure erased them. She looked even younger than she was — about twelve years old.

It was during this journey up the California coast that he managed with mild persistence to get her to talk about herself. She was married, she said, to a former neighbour, Jim Dougherty, who was in the Merchant Marines. The wedding had taken place two weeks after her sixteenth birthday. She had worked in a war plant assembly line packing parachutes and won a much-prized 'E for Excellence' certificate for her efforts. An Army photographer, David Conover, had taken her picture for a feature on women in war work for *Yank* magazine. This had led to a few more magazine sessions but nothing more had come of her hopes of a modelling career. An introduction to Emmeline Snively had led to jobs as a hostess at various industrial trade shows, where pretty girls traditionally stand around the exhibits and smile a lot.

With her twentieth birthday looming in a matter of weeks — the beginning of June — she was beginning to feel an urgency about her career. 'It wasn't that she asked outright for help. There was just something about her that made you *want* to help,' says Jasgur. This was a reaction that was to be felt by legions of men and women who entered her orbit over the years, her in-born magnetic pull on the emotional heartstrings of otherwise prudent and rational people.

Jasgur is frank to admit that he did not see a star-studded future for Norma Jean Dougherty. There was no epiphany, no rockets went off in his mind. 'I thought she could be reasonably successful as a model; I liked her. I wanted to help her. And remember, I was a young guy with a lot of energy, a lot of cameras and a big Lincoln coupé. What could be more fun than spending the day at the beach taking pictures?'

It wasn't until 41 years later when Joseph Jasgur was alone in his darkroom making prints of that day's excursion that he noticed something odd about Norma Jean's left foot. She had six toes. A surprising discovery, he thought, but not earth-shaking. He had heard rumours of plastic surgery on her foot as well as her nose and chin, but he notes, 'It's none of my business.'

His business that day at Zuma Beach was to bring Norma Jean out of her shell. 'Draw a heart in the sand!' he directed.

An inexplicable shyness overwhelmed her. She shook her head no and sat down on the beach, arms crossed, a sad expression on her face. What deep emotional pain had he triggered, Joe wondered.

'Just a small heart. With your fingertip. It's easy. Try it,' he wheedled.

Not looking at him, she managed to trace out a small quivery heart shape.

'See? You can do it!'

The gloom bubble popped. Her face and body freed themselves from whatever demons had invaded them. With a radiant smile and laughing eyes, she drew a perfectly shaped enormous heart on the hard wet sand. 'This is for you, Joe darling!' — the first sign of the mischievous side of her nature. A moment later, amid the good-natured congratulations for her artistic triumph, she quite suddenly stamped out the heart with her foot and walked away.

A few more shots and Joe was ready to pack up his equipment and head back to the studio. Norma Jean changed back into the pink sweater and checked pedal-pushers she had worn the first day she had appeared in his doorway. What a difference these few short weeks had made in their relationship. The quiet reserve had cracked open like an eggshell to expose the slowly emerging fluffball of a chick.

'...In spite of the fact that she wasn't terribly attractive to look at, she usually came out extremely well in photographs...'

Elliot Erwitt

Getting her to draw the heart in the sand and stick out her tongue had somehow triggered the zany aspect of her personality which would ultimately express itself in her high comedy performances in *The Seven Year Itch* and *Some Like it Hot*. On this spring afternoon in 1946, however, she contented herself by turning the tables on Joe Jasgur.

'Just one more!' she insisted, mimicking the phrase all photographers use, whether shooting heads of state or beauty queen winners. 'Roll up your pants, Joe!' Again mimicking his commanding tone of voice, only now she was the parent, he the child. 'Let's compare legs. Let's see whose legs are better.'

The silliness of it all proved to be a perfect ending to a glorious afternoon. They laughed and sang all the way back to Joe's studio. That night with her beside him in the darkroom as he developed and printed the day's efforts, their relationship heightened. Previously she had been skittish in the close confines of the darkroom, girding herself for what she expected to be a demand of sexual payment for the test shots.

'That's not how I operated,' Joe explains. 'And as soon as she realized this was so, she relaxed with me, knowing she could be affectionate without my taking advantage of her.'

A week later, they returned to Zuma Beach. To add to the fun, he had invited three members of the the cast of a local production of a time-worn melodrama *The Drunkard* to join them in costume. The idea, Joe explained, was to improvise, get everyone in a good mood and see what happened. When Norma Jean changed into her swimsuit, the change in her was equally dramatic, as if someone had clicked on her energy switch. She raced across the sand to the water's edge and back again like a demented wind-up toy, exulting in the sea air on her bare skin and the feeling of powdery sand between her toes.

In a little while, a cool breeze came up from the sea. Norma Jean, in her favourite bird bathing suit, had said almost nothing to Joe and the others. As if to make amends, she asked Joe if she could wear his jacket and then insisted he set up his camera on a timer so that the group could all be photographed together.

'It was she who put my arm around her shoulder as a way of saying she was sorry. With her arm behind my back, I felt this was a show of trust and friendship. I could feel her close to me and I

'God gave her everything. The first day a photographer took a picture of her she was a genius.'

Maurice Zolotow

remember an amazing thing. Instead of feeling sexy, I felt proud of this special kind of intimacy. And I felt happy.'

This night and the days and nights that followed were a happy time for Joseph Jasgur. Although their physical relationship was limited to horseplay – the hugs and kisses and wrestling of adolescents which Norma Jean had clearly never experienced – Joe's deepest gratification came from seeing how quickly she learned the tricks of interacting with the camera.

'But that's the way it was,' Joe says simply. 'If I had known she was going to be famous, I'd have taken many more pictures of her! But as for having an affair, I'm an old-fashioned kind of guy – strange as that may sound. She was married. Her husband was away in the Merchant Marines, serving his country. Maybe nobody will believe this, especially with the sexual revolution and all that's happened since the Forties, but I couldn't see myself going after somebody else's wife.'

He treasures the memories of their private times together, in the darkroom, driving places in his convertible, and sitting in the back row at the movies. 'We'd have popcorn and whisper in the dark. She'd nibble on my ear and kiss me on the cheek. And what she liked best was to cuddle like a homeless kitten or puppy.'

As springtime advanced toward summer, Norma Jean became an integral part of Joe Jasgur's life. He photographed her in various settings. One such session was on the grounds of the Ambassador Hotel along with other young members of Emmeline's Hollywood Blue Book models catalogue. Joe admits to playing favourites. He saw to it that Norma Jean was the centre of attention. In keeping with the pin-up conventions of the period, he dolled her up in a peasant blouse, teamed her up with a friendly Dalmatian and got her to braid her hair across the top of her head *fräulein* style for a milk-fed country-girl look.

Another popular convention was the farmer's daughter ideal. Joe assembled an idyllic 'farmyard' scene and dressed Norma Jean in rolled-up denim shorts, a plaid shirt and square-dance straw hat. 'You see how chunky she was?' Jasgur beams with satisfaction. 'The girls today are much too thin.'

All during this time, Emmeline Snively was making connections for Norma Jean to audition for a film contract. The studio system was still very much in effect. Television had not yet changed things. Scores of promising young women were signed to short-term contracts and given training while the moguls decided what – if anything – to do with them.

Norma Jean was excited by the possibility of a film career and Joe Jasgur was excited for her, although he didn't have too much hope for her success. 'I did what I could to help her,' he admits.

She needed eight-by-ten prints of his photographs. He made as many as she needed and as often as she needed them. He never charged her for them, he admits with a wry smile, and she never offered payment. The only suggestion of disappointment concerns the disappearance of six transparencies. 'Norma Jean borrowed them one day on some pretext or other. I'm sure she meant to return them but she never did. I've never seen them printed anywhere so I can only assume they were accidentally thrown away.' The thought of these 'lost' images stashed away in some forgotten file drawer or cardboard box makes him smile.

'Somebody's in for a big surprise someday!'

As the weeks went by, Joe and Norma Jean fell into a friendly routine of getting together on an informal basis. 'They weren't dates. She'd either show up in Jim Dougherty's old convertible or maybe I'd call her and see if she wanted to tag along with me on my night-club rounds,' he says. Because his photographs of celebrities at play appeared regularly in fan magazines and newspapers, he was warmly welcomed at such famous watering holes as the Mocambo, Ciro's, the Brown Derby and the Trocadero.

These excursions were her introduction to the glamorous places where she herself would later be photographed. As Joe's 'assistant', she carried the bag containing film and flashbulbs. The lush surroundings and lavishly dressed people intimidated her. She stuck closely to Joe's side. 'Would you believe it? Here was Marilyn Monroe, or at least the future Marilyn Monroe, right in their midst and not one man made a play for her. Not one of them asked to be introduced or tried to get her phone number.'

It was on one of these nights that Norma Jean said, 'I've got something wonderful to tell you, Joe.'

'It's Jean Harlow all over again.'

Ben Lyon

Into the Lyon's Den

Through a contact of Emmeline's, Norma Jean had arranged an appointment to meet the famous Ben Lyon, casting director at 20th Century-Fox. Dapper, witty and handsome, Lyon was a star in his own right – both of the silents and the early talkies, and of the stage. He was best known, perhaps, for his marriage to actress and singer Bebe Daniels, for together they were the cinema screen's most popular married couple. American born, Bebe and Ben would later become Anglo-Americans during the war, living and working in London and giving to both countries a friendship which would never be forgotten. Many remember Ben and Bebe for their unforgettable, long-running radio and then television programmes – 'Life with the Lyons' – a family-oriented, live show featuring Ben and Bebe with their children Richard and Barbara. A skilled pilot for many years, Lyon also served with distinction in the RAF as a combat pilot during the war, achieving the rank of Lieutenant Colonel.

But it was after the heady days of his British success that Ben Lyon met Norma Jean. Famous for discovering another silver-screen blonde, Jean Harlow, Lyon was the step on to the ladder that Norma Jean was looking for.

Virtually unheralded, Norma Jean walked into Lyon's office and he was, like Jasgur, aware of that *something* she had. 'From the moment that Norma Jean Dougherty walked into my office I was certain she had star qualities,' he said. 'She came in at eleven a.m., and within one hour I signed her to a seven-year optional contract ... At six p.m. that day we tested her in colour and within a week exercised our option on her services.'

Norma Jean told Joe breathlessly that his portfolio of photographs were responsible for Lyon's agreeing to see her. 'See how important you are to me, Joe? Why don't we get married?' she joked, her excitement evident.

The day of her interview with Ben Lyon, Jasgur kept busy until the appointed time. Then he could do nothing but watch the clock and wait for the phone to ring. At last, there she was, a laughing and crying Norma Jean. 'He loved me. He loved your photographs. He says I'll be the new Jean Harlow!' Nothing was definite yet, but Norma Jean had no doubt about what lay ahead. And Lyon was impressed by the budding starlet: 'She was the most conscientious youngster signed by the company,' he noted later. 'She devoted all her time to study, training and exercise so that when an opportunity came she would be prepared. I have the greatest admiration for her.'

'When she walked on stage, she stood out so much that nobody looked at anybody else.'

Bill McLean

Over a celebratory dinner at an intimate little restaurant called the Spanish Kitchen, Norma Jean said Ben Lyon did not like her name. Norma Jean Dougherty was not a suitable name for a film star. Emmeline had come to the same conclusion earlier, and suggested Jean Norman as a possibility – it was as Jean Norman that Norma Jean would do much of her work at the Blue Book agency.

Jasgur takes no credit for changing Norma Jean Dougherty to Marilyn Monroe. 'It was all Ben Lyon's idea.' Following that first interview, Ben Lyon kept his word. After all, it was he who had talked producer Howard Hughes into hiring Jean Harlow as Lyon's co-star in the award-winning *Hell's Angels*. He knew that Fox studio boss Darryl Zanuck was partial to blondes. This newcomer, if handled right, could be the next Betty Grable.

Working secretly, without head office authority, Lyon had arranged for wardrobe, hairdressing and make-up. His close friend, the noted director Walter Lang, had agreed to shoot some colour footage after hours. The one hundred feet of silent film more than justified Lyon's behaviour. Great showman that he was, the casting director slipped the test footage into Zanuck's projection room among the 'dailies' and other screen tests. Within a few days, Zanuck gave Lyon the green light to use Norma Jean Dougherty. She had been signed to a seven-year contract – at a starting salary of seventy-five dollars a week, with renewable six-month options providing a twenty-five dollar increase each time, rising to a ceiling of $1500 dollars during the seventh year. In other words, the seven-year contract could be dropped by the studio after any given six-month period, but Norma Jean could not break the agreement at any time.

Not that she cared. Ben Lyon was her new saviour and mentor. He and his wife welcomed her to their home and took a warm and loving interest in her career, attention she had up to then relied on Joe to give her. Lyon and Bebe left for London before Marilyn had achieved her sought-after success. Before he left, Ben assured that she was put forward for a number of parts. As a 20th Century-Fox studio executive said, 'He helped her get roles – no matter how small.' Many years later, when Ben returned to Hollywood to meet the now famous star, she grew emotional, showing her appreciation by signing a photograph of herself with the words:

> *You found me, named me and believed in me when no one else did.*
> *My love and thanks forever.*

The Lyon-Monroe friendship lasted until her death.

Several days after her meeting with Lyon, and the signature of her contracts, Norma Jean called Joe with the good news and suggested they have dinner.

'Guess what my new name is?'

He couldn't.

'Marilyn Monroe!' she pursed her lips. '*M-m-m!*'

Ben Lyon had suggested 'Marilyn', a name to which he had sentimental attachment, as a tribute to Marilyn Miller, the famous Broadway musical comedy star of the Twenties. Norma Jean reminded him of that other famous blonde, who had once starred with him in a movie. It was a coincidence that Norma Jean would become Marilyn Miller herself, following her marriage to Arthur Miller in 1956. 'Monroe' turned out to be Norma Jean's idea, in honour of her mother's mother, Della Monroe Grainger, who died a few months after Norma Jean's first birthday.

That dinner in the summer of 1946 marked the end of Norma Jean and the birth of Marilyn

Monroe. 'I guess you could say I was the last person to see Norma Jean before she disappeared forever,' says Jasgur.

It took him a long while to realize she had cut him out of her life. 'A surgical amputation and I didn't feel a thing until weeks later. I should have got the message right away, but I didn't.

'At the end of the evening, I kissed her good night and like always I said, "Speak to you tomorrow." When I thought of it later, she looked kind of funny. She said she knew I would understand that with the new contract and all she was going to be pretty busy; she wouldn't be having much free time so it was going to be hard to get together.'

The memory of what turned out to be their final moments together clouds his eyes. It still hurts. 'She kissed me on the cheek and said she was sure I would understand.'

'Like John Wayne and a few other giants, she had a star quality that had nothing to do with acting.'

Ben Lyon

The Sweet Taste of Success

Joe admits to having been naïve. It took several weeks of broken dates and abrupt phone calls to make him understand that Norma Jean had gone forever — from his world as well as her own. In her place was a newborn fully grown woman called Marilyn Monroe who had no place in her life for a photographer named Joseph Jasgur.

Not that she became a star overnight. There were still two years of hard times and hard knocks before bit parts in three totally forgettable films led to a hip-swinging encounter with Groucho Marx in *Love Happy* (1950) and her immortal line: 'Men keep following me.'

The mythology that evolved about the genesis of her famous 'swivel walk' makes Jasgur hoot with laughter. 'A lot of baloney has been written about it. One so-called expert swore that she cut a half inch off the heel of one shoe. Would you believe it?'

The truth was more mundane. She suffered from a congenital defect of the knees called hyper-extension. In other words, she was double-jointed and, when she walked, her knees would click in and out of their sockets causing her buttocks to sway from side to side.

After the first hurtful months of separation, he gave up trying to reach or see her. She never phoned him or dropped by the studio unannounced as she had previously.

'Time wounds all heels!' Jasgur jokes. He was much in demand not only as a celebrity photographer but as a gritty photo-journalist covering such notorious Hollywood crime cases as the Black Dahlia murder. His Lincoln custom coupé was equipped with the most up-to-the-minute gadgetry: a police radio and siren, mobile telephones, a 110-volt electric system so he could shave while driving, and a back seat that converted into a bed so he could have a quick snooze during stake-outs.

By 1950, Marilyn Monroe was not exactly a household name. Jasgur had by that time put her and her earlier incarnation, Norma Jean Dougherty, out of his mind when suddenly there she was in the living flesh just a few feet away from him and his ever-present camera. The occasion was the 1950 Players Ball at the Pantages Theater. Joe was on assignment for the *Hollywood Citizen-News* as usual and had taken his position at the entrance to the theatre to shoot the various celebrities as they arrived for a picture spread in the next day's paper.

'Mickey Rooney was the top box-office star at the time. When his limousine pulled up and

'...a young lady who can walk by me in such a manner as to arouse my elderly libido, and cause smoke to issue from my ears.'

Groucho Marx

stopped, we all jockeyed for the best angle. The press paid little attention to his date. He liked to show up at public events with a gorgeous babe on his arm. This night was no exception. The babe was blonde, beautiful, curvaceous and looked as if she had been poured into her skin-tight dress. As she clung to Mickey's arm, pressing her face close to his in order to ensure being included in the photographs, Jasgur realized it was Norma Jean. 'Correction, Marilyn Monroe. I was so happy to see her looking so beautiful and glamorous,' he remembers.

Moving swiftly toward her and her diminutive escort, Joe started to call her Norma Jean until he remembered Norma Jean no longer existed. 'Marilyn? This way, please. Give us a smile.' So certain was he that she would recognize him and greet him like the long-lost friend he was that he kept up the photographer's banter as a kind of personal joke between them. Any second now he expected her to laugh and call out to him in her whispery voice, 'Joe, darlin'. How are you?'

When she gave no sign of recognition, he thought she might not want to annoy Mickey by having a conversation with a photographer. Following the pair inside the Pantages, he sidled up to her. 'Hi, Marilyn. Remember me?' He didn't mean it literally. It was the kind of question old friends ask in long-time-no-see situations.

She looked him straight in the eye without a glimmer of recognition. 'No. I don't think I do. Who are you?' she said calmly.

Still clinging to the idea that she must be kidding or had some reason for stiffing him, he persisted in a teasing tone, 'Don't you remember Joe Jasgur, the guy who took all those pictures of you, the pictures Ben Lyon liked so much he signed you to a contract?'

'I don't think I do,' she said and turned her back.

Her behaviour still puzzles him. Hearing that she cut off other people did little to assuage his own hurt. For a few weeks he couldn't let the situation rest. He placed many phone calls and left several messages. She never called him back. Their conversation in the lobby of the Pantages Theater was the last time he ever spoke to her.

'Hollywood is a town based on hurt feelings.' He shrugs carelessly but his voice trembles. 'It was a close friendship for a very short time. What's gone is gone. You learn to live with it.'

How did he feel years later when she became a sex goddess and a superstar? 'That was Marilyn Monroe, the entirely new person she had created. The woman I knew was Norma Jean, a little chubby, a little shy and very brave. I can only guess that Norma Jean remained at the core of the sleek and sassy Marilyn but I never had the chance to find out.'

Calendar Girl

Photographer Tom Kelley was a friend and colleague of Joe's. In 1946 he asked Marilyn to pose nude, but she declined. Three years later, however, when she had been dropped by 20th Century-Fox and Columbia, she agreed to do the shots — for fifty dollars. Kelley's wife Natalie helped with the shoot, and the couple became friends with the out-of-work actress. In a weak attempt at anonymity, Marilyn signed her release forms with the alias 'Mona Monroe', but her secret was short-lived.

In 1952, a reporter learned that the famous 'Golden Dreams' calendar girl was Marilyn Monroe, the rising star of the 20th Century-Fox stable, where she had been re-signed. Kelley's 'Golden Dreams' nude of Marilyn Monroe posed against red velvet caused a further uproar when the United States postal authorities threatened to ban it as pornography. And when word leaked out about the identity of the model, Marilyn's career nearly came to a full stop because of the morals clause in her contract. Wise heads prevailed. The publicity was worth millions and overnight made her a household name.

'I've done nothing wrong,' she said firmly. 'I was broke and I needed the money.' Reports later called it the single most effective publicity feat in show business history, for *Clash by Night*, her first major film opened to great box-office success. In 1982, Joseph Jasgur ran into Tom Kelley at an exhibition commemorating the twentieth anniversary of Marilyn's death. The work of both photographers was on prominent display. As the two friends reminisced about the old days in Hollywood, Tom recalled meeting Norma Jean in 1947. She had become Marilyn Monroe by then, but lots of people still called her Norma Jean. He remembered thinking she didn't look very photogenic — until she showed him her Joe Jasgur prints.

Would Jasgur ever have photographed her in the nude? The question is one he cannot bring himself easily to answer. He is a man of courtly old-fashioned values. He pulls out chairs for women. He opens car doors. His sense of courtesy is such that when a question is asked he feels an obligation to answer. He clears his throat and begins by saying how much he respects and admires Tom Kelley's work and considers his Marilyn nude a work of rare beauty and sensitivity. As for Norma Jean, 'I never gave it a thought. It never entered my mind. If a nude session was ever going to happen it would have happened much, much later. I could not have ever said, "Take off your clothes, Norma Jean" during the time we were together. It was much too soon for her.'

'When she posed nude, it was "Gee, I am kind of, you know, sort of dishy", like she enjoyed it without being egotistical.'

Elizabeth Taylor

The Girl in the Old-Fashioned Bathing Costume

Mary Lou Massey remembers it well — that glorious day at Zuma Beach with Joseph Jasgur, Norma Jean Dougherty and friends from the cast of *The Drunkard*, the old-fashioned melodrama about the evils of alcohol. Mary Lou was another of Emmeline Snively's Hollywood Blue Book models, and she and Norma Jean were often sent out on assignment together. The girl in the polka dot swimming costume in the picture on page 84 is Mary Lou. Forty years later she easily recalls that day.

'Norma Jean was blonde; I was brunette. We were the same size for modelling clothes so we were a good combination.'

In contrast to later reports of being late and impossible to work with, Mary Lou remembers Norma Jean as being sweet, dear and reliable. 'A shy person, a darling girl. You'd have enjoyed being with her. I don't know what Hollywood did to her.'

Although the two young women often had lunch together, Norma Jean always avoided discussing her private thoughts. 'She didn't go in for the usual girl talk. You know, clothes, make-up, love, all the things that interested girls our age. She didn't enjoy talking about them.'

It was as if Norma Jean had erected an invisible wall around her emotions to keep everyone out. She didn't talk much about her husband because she knew he didn't approve of her ambitions and was jealous of her posing for photographers. In any case, Norma Jean had, at first, hidden the fact of her marriage from Emmeline Snively because in those days the 'girl-next-door' image was supposed to be 'innocent' as well as seductive. Since Jim Dougherty was away at sea most of the time, his presence

'She was awkward. She couldn't get out of her own way. She wasn't disciplined, and she was often late ... she seemed just a carefree kid, and she owned the world.'

Barbara Stanwyck

was never an issue.

Norma Jean rarely mentioned him — nor at that time did she appear to have any other love interest. Her concentration was focused on her career. She felt very comfortable with Joseph Jasgur because he was a gentleman and treated her with respect.

A few months after their day at Zuma Beach, Norma Jean's contract with 20th Century-Fox changed her life completely, and Mary Lou never saw her again. Her own life was caught up in a whirlwind of change as well. As a romantic footnote to the Zuma Beach photo session, she eventually married Tom Burton, her debonair moustachioed co-star in *The Drunkard*, who had joined that day's fun in a striped turn-of-the-century bathing costume. When Tom died he left Mary Lou with two little girls to support

A brief show-business career followed. She and her husband formed a musical group. In addition to being a singer and dancer, she was one of the first under-water ballet swimmers, and later taught Esther Williams some of her early techniques.

Today Mary Lou lives with her second husband Millard Massey far from Hollywood in Northern California, not far from Sutter's Fort where gold was discovered in 1848 and the California Gold Rush began. 'Life has treated us well,' she recalls. 'We're comfortable and happy. We don't miss the Hollywood high life.'

She thinks Norma Jean would have enjoyed visiting with them. The peacefulness and quiet, the awesome beauty of the mountains and wildlife may have eased the tensions that tormented and ultimately destroyed her.

As for the scurrilous attacks on Marilyn Monroe, Mary Lou is her staunch and outspoken defender. 'If someone makes a nasty remark, I don't let them get away with it. She was a dear and loving person.'

At this point, Mary Lou chokes up for a moment. When she continues it is in a voice that pleads for attention to one essential point that is never mentioned.

'Keep in mind, Norma Jean never played a mean person. She couldn't play a mean person because it wasn't in her to be mean.'

With a final, heart-felt sigh, Mary Lou concludes, 'I wish her well. I believe in the hereafter. Maybe one day I'll be able to tell her that.'

All Alone on a Saturday Night

Westwood is one of the hundreds of villages and towns which comprise the Greater Los Angeles area. Bordering the University of California campus and a Bohemian staging area for artists, musicians, and film-makers, it is a high-decibel fusion of cinemas, takeaway joints, disc and video stores, and street stalls selling T-shirts and biodegradable crafts. In sharp contrast to its boisterous lifestyle is the Westwood Mortuary and Memorial Park where the earthly remains of Marilyn Monroe are sequestered in a wall vault on the left side as you come through the entrance. Although the cemetery is quite literally just a few yards south of Wilshire Boulevard, and two streets away from the bustle and speed of the San Diego Freeway, it is a verdant oasis of tranquillity.

Joseph Jasgur shows me the simple marker:

'She could have made it with a little luck.'

Arthur Miller

MARILYN MONROE
1926 –1962

On this particular day, the attendant vase contains a tender handful of field flowers, predominantly daisies. The attached card, written with a shaky hand, reads: *'Peace on Earth. We love you, Marilyn. Your fan —'* Instead of a signature, there is a drawing of a face with a sad smile.

Another item of Marilyn mythology surfaces. Wasn't it true that Joe DiMaggio sent red roses three times a week and often paid his respects in person? A mortuary official declined to comment. As far as Joseph Jasgur knows, the roses did arrive on a regular basis for years and continue to be among the many floral tributes that arrive each August on the anniversary of her death.

How did he feel that day in August 1962 when he heard of her death? As it happened, he was a patient in a Los Angeles hospital preparing for surgery. His initial reaction was utter disbelief. 'I was shocked and surprised and deeply saddened. I never believed all those theories of murder and conspiracy. I still don't. Marilyn Monroe was not the Norma Jean I knew sixteen years before. All I can say is I sensed that Norma Jean was afraid of growing old and of being alone. And there she was, the sex goddess of every man's erotic dreams all alone, all by herself on a Saturday night when the rest of the world was making love and having fun.'

On Reflection

Meeting Joseph Jasgur, I can understand why Norma Jean felt comfortable with him. Trim, agile and looking decades younger than his seventy-one years, he exudes an aura of gentle humour and genuine courtesy. Although he has lived and worked in Southern California for half a century, his voice reflects his mid-west roots, a kind of easy-going Henry Fonda cadence that makes you feel you've known him all your life.

His features, though weathered by the passage of forty-five years since he compared legs with Norma Jean on the beach at Malibu, are instantly recognizable – the way some people's baby pictures preview the adult. His eyes are merry and direct, his mouth ready to grin. His hair, not surprisingly, is a bit thinner and greyer, a fact he blithely covered up with a rakish cap that says:

FOCUS
FOCUS
FOCUS

'That's my motto!' he explains. 'Focus on whatever you're doing while you're doing it.'

We are tucking into a Californian health breakfast of succulent fresh fruit: kiwi, raspberries, blueberries and sliced bananas; ripe dates and a mélange of walnuts and muesli with a splash of low-fat skimmed milk. 'The California lifestyle. That's what keeps me going,' he says.

We are in the restaurant of the Westwood Marquis. The atmosphere zings with the tensions at nearby tables. Deals, and deals to make deals, are being made. The Hollywood 'trades', *Daily Variety,*

'This atrocious death will be a terrible lesson for those whose principal occupation consists of spying on and tormenting the film stars.'

Jean Cocteau

the *Hollywood Reporter* and *Billboard* grace every table along with scripts, treatments, CDs, video tapes and other showbiz status symbols.

When I set up my tape recorder for our interview, there is a perceptible though subtle response. Innocent glances flicker in our direction. The waiter with the coffee carafe hovers with attention. The basket of muffins and multi-grain breads is offered again and again.

Joe and I recognize the scenario. There's no need to discuss it. We accept our roles and play out our parts, I the pale visitor in East Coast clothes interviewing the dynamic older man who looks vaguely familiar and could be an old-time mogul or director, or, in the local argot, 'somebody'.

Clearly, he is enjoying our talk about Norma Jean and what their times together were like. The added, unexpected pleasure is the mild stir of curiosity we are exciting by our presence. Joseph Jasgur knows full well that he is *somebody*. He is comfortable with himself and proud of his accomplishments. If people approve, he's delighted. If not, he couldn't care less.

Other Faces ... Other Blondes

In the quixotic world of celebrity, blondes come, blondes go. Some are remembered in a golden nimbus of nostalgia; others sink like a stone in a bottomless pit. The early film blondes, Mary Pickford, the Gish sisters and Mae West surface regularly in vintage film fests. Jean Harlow, the first bleached blonde, wisecracked her way into men's arms and fans' hearts, followed by Carole Lombard (sassy), Betty Grable (cute as a button), Lana Turner (sultry) and Veronica Lake (hard-boiled).

Jayne Mansfield, Anita Ekberg, Diana Dors and Kim Novak bared as much of their bosoms as the sex police would allow, while a pouting Brigitte Bardot turned the tables and her back, baring her bottom with kittenish insouciance.

There was Doris Day, the freckle-faced hoyden sublimating her ardour until wedding bells rang and white-gloved ice maidens like Grace Kelly and Eva Marie Saint, flaring their nostrils in erotic expectation. More recently, the more sexually forthright Julie Christie, Faye Dunaway, Jessica Lange and Cybil Shepherd began to show the rest of us a thing or two about fancy frolicking.

Currently, blondes have acquired a new stature. Michelle Pfeiffer, Glenn Close and Meryl Streep are worshipped as much for their acting ability as for their physical impact. For the most part, journalists have stopped drawing too-easy parallels between them and Marilyn Monroe with one exception.

Madonna.

Yet, Madonna soon overthrew the blonde bombshell impersonation when she received the same scepticism from the Press about her abilities that Marilyn had faced. Even today, while Madonna can play the part, it's clear that it must be viewed as a humorous send-up, that tougher stuff lurks beneath.

Blondes come and go. Other, newer blondes are being born or made. Yet Marilyn prevails. As the twenty-first century looms, her image remains omnipresent. She is everywhere, all around us, in books, videos, posters, greeting cards, on T-shirts, and in museums. The Marilyn impersonator is the keystone of camp. A Marilyn Monroe white wine began as a hype and continues to sell well in America for a simple reason. It tastes great. A memorabilia collector recently paid Christie's New York over four million dollars for Andy Warhol's 1964 portrait, 'Shot Red Marilyn'. An autographed 1952 pin-up photograph of her in a lacy black negligée inscribed, 'To Carol, the best always', fetched four thousand dollars from an ordinary fan. At the 1991 Autograph Show in New York, dealers said one Marilyn Monroe signature is worth ten of George Bush's.

The now classic photograph of her standing over the subway grate in *The Seven Year Itch* has been further immortalized in a collectable plate offered in a limited edition. Almost thirty years after her death, her face and figure abound in student bedrooms, locker rooms and on the walls of neighbourhood bistros, beauty parlours and launderettes. If there's a wall, there's almost certain to be a Marilyn.

On a recent stroll down Rodeo Drive, the exclusive fashion boulevard of Beverly Hills, a crowd of normally blasé shoppers pressed against the window of Gianni Versace's salon. What they were looking at was a seductive portrait of Marilyn Monroe in full pout emblazoned in vivid colour on a custom ensemble. The price? A resounding $2700.

As a cult figure, she resigns supreme. There is and will continue to be only one Marilyn. For Joseph Jasgur, there was only one Norma Jean. More than anything else, he hopes she, too, will be remembered.

'Unique is an over-worked word, but in her case it applies. There will never be another like her, and Lord knows there have been plenty of imitations.'

Billy Wilder

The Eternal Orphan

Jasgur's photographs haunt me. They break my heart. She's so vulnerable. She's all the little girls at the orphans' picnic rolled into one, determined to make an ordinary occasion glamorous and sophisticated. She's so proud to be singled out, to be the focus of attention. She wants you to notice her and invite her into your life. Looking at these early awkward poses, it's hard to believe that in a few years she'd be marrying two of America's legendary men, co starring with the world's greatest classical actor and shaking hands with the Queen of England.

Accepting 1946 as the year Marilyn Monroe was born, it's intriguing to see how the stories of her ante-natal years as Norma Jean vary. There are her subsequent memories after she became Marilyn, confided to others who in turn interpreted and embroidered the details for even more dramatic effect. There are the skewed reminiscences of some who actually knew her pre-1946 but had no way of knowing she would be famous and therefore did not make notes. And then there are the indirect chroniclers who came across a copy of a copy of a copy of an original copy of an anecdote that has been told, retold, edited, changed and emerges distorted.

If you've ever played Chinese Whispers, you know what can happen. A sentence whispered to one person travels and changes as it is whispered to the next person who in turn whispers it to the next. Hearing is selective. Listeners 'choose' the parts they like and ignore the rest. By the time the sixth or seventh person down the line gets the message it bears little resemblance to the original.

So many millions of words have been written about her, it's easy to wonder why she didn't set the record straight and tell it like it was in her own autobiography. While she may well have assumed she had plenty of time for that — after all, you don't expect to die at thirty-six — it's my guess she would never have been able to tell the story of her early years. The 'true' facts were too painful. She had erased some from her memory tape and candy-coated others so they could be endured. In her first studio bio, she said both parents had died in a car crash and only later under pressure of fact did she

'There's more to Marilyn than meets the eye. The trouble is that when people look at her they immediately figure her as a typical Hollywood Blonde. It's not just their fault, though. Marilyn's soul just doesn't fit her body.'

Natasha Lytess

admit her mother Gladys was alive, if not well, in a mental institution.

In one sense, Marilyn Monroe gave birth to herself in 1946 and became as much her own mother has her own child. Josh White once sang, '*I was born one morning 'bout the break of day/I took my burden and I walked away*'. Marilyn took her burden and started down the lonesome road.

I've reviewed the literature of her early years, the books, clippings, recollections. I've sifted through the records of what she said about her past, present and plans for the future. The Press was not called the media in the late Forties and Fifties, that slender slot of time between the Second World War and rock 'n' roll. Movie magazines and Hollywood columnists had created a separate fanzine world of hard-working stars devoted to their art but also seeking true love.

Norma Jean had grown up reading the emotionally charged articles about Jean Harlow, Joan Crawford, Carole Lombard, Betty Grable, Rita Hayworth and other reigning goddesses and their private passions, dreams, fears and tragedies. When her turn came, she was self-programmed. She knew exactly what was expected of a starlet on the rise, exactly how to style Marilyn Monroe as the orphan sexpot who read Walt Whitman, kept a portrait of Abraham Lincoln at her bedside and wanted more than anything to have six children and a real home.

From the evidence assembled, she conducted her life, her friendships, her love affairs, her marriages and her career like one long extended fan magazine interview. The reason may be this: there was never a core centre or a sense of continuity in her Norma Jean life. There was nobody to remember things with her or for her. Her father a mysterious blur if that, her mother a muddled prisoner of her own emotional demons. Norma Jean was a cork afloat on treacherous seas. Every so often, a wind shift tossed her ashore to some temporary harbour only to sweep back in when least expected. She had to use all her strength and will power to stay afloat and keep from drowning. Like a cork, she might be swamped but she refused to sink. However battered and alone, she insisted on surviving.

Stars like Ginger Rogers and Lauren Bacall had mothers to encourage their ambitions, praise their beauty and talents and give behind-the-scenes support to their careers. Norma Jean was alone. Through the horrors of the Thirties Depression, girls her age endured poverty in the bosom of tightly-knit families. Norma Jean had no immediate family to count on for the goodnight kiss or morning hug. She had to face the terrors of childhood by herself in the only way she could, through fantasy and the single-minded rage to *be* somebody.

What she most wanted and never found was a family. Cheated of her own by circumstances, she spent her life looking for kinfolk she could trust and a real home where she could relax and be part of a family, like the kind in the *Saturday Evening Post*. She sought mothering from everyone — men, women, lovers, friends, producers, directors, writers, photographers and the Hollywood Press. She wanted a universal embrace of maternal cosseting, a fluffy chick under a protective wing, giving her the courage to go forth into the Hollywood world.

Her search by definition was doomed. She yearned for a mythical mothering which is not characterized by gender but rather by nurturing. She hungered for a 'mother's' guidance on what to wear, how to improve herself and the best way to impress strangers. With no real mother to guide her, she was forever — and until the terrible Saturday night of her death — destiny's dark angel, desperately reaching out for the illusory figure who would be consistently caring, approving and loyal no matter what the naughty child in her did to test this devotion.

She was the eternal orphan, wounded beyond healing, her nose pressed to life's window, pleading, 'Let me in . . . ' She wanted paternal, nurturing men. She enjoyed her power to excite men sexually but more than that she wanted to be Daddy's girl. To her, marriage seemed to mean captivating a man and moving into his circle. She avoided being the lady of the house in her own right. She was a visitor on a pass. Her sexual magnetism got her into other people's homes through the kind of 'good' behaviour society secretly considered bad. In her romances and marriages, she strove to be both the sexpot and a member of an extended family who helped wash the dishes and play with the children.

In history, politics and love, there is no such thing as absolute truth. In film-making there is the POV or Point of View, which is what the director arbitrarily chooses for us to see and feel. POV in life as in film is a totally subjective and personal narrow focus. In a way, it's like watching sports on television. We don't see everything that's happening in the stadium or arena. We see what the TV director chooses to show us.

We will never know all that happened to Marilyn. She could not always separate humiliating fact from necessary fiction. Her POV focused narrowly on what she wanted to see, editing out and discarding the rest.

The plethora of information about her early days is usually ambiguous and factually inaccurate. Rather than seek the one elusive truth about her past – or creation – I gave in to the realization that fact is subjective at best. Watch the evening news in Britain, you see one version of events; watch the same thing in America or Europe or Asia and you get a different POV.

During the gestation and birth of Marilyn Monroe, there were many midwives, both men and women. Some have died or disappeared; some are still around, their POV tempered by how life has subsequently treated them. Some memories have softened with time, others have crusted over. Some peripheral people have declared themselves in – in one way or another.

Misremembering Marilyn is chronic. Given the chance to speak out, it's tempting to move centre stage and be a Proustian footnote in a remembrance of things past – or flings past, as the case may be. Oleg Cassini tells about meeting Marilyn in 1947 and inviting her home to a fancy party his wife Gene Tierney was throwing. Cassini somehow forgot to mention the invitation to Gene. He recalls, 'Marilyn was the first to arrive, creating waves of sexual turbulence in her immediate vicinity, leaving quivering eddies of desire in her wake.' The infuriated Tierney called her a tramp. Within a few months, the Cassinis separated, although not specifically over Marilyn. His description of her remains one of the most charming. She was a starlet then but Cassini saw the qualities that had universal appeal: 'the sweetness, vulnerability, the curious triple-edged naïveté, at once innocent, encouraging and gently mocking of male desire. This was not just another body walking around; there was a brain attached.'

Cassini is one of the many post-mortem confessors of carnally knowing Marilyn. Ever continental of manner, he spares us the sweaty details, simply recalling, 'one thing led to another . . . indeed, the dénouement had been inevitable from the moment she entered the room.' He adds chivalrously, 'She was quite wonderful.'

Cassini is a gent. Other men have retroactively declared themselves 'in', years after the fact – like war veterans chorusing 'I was there'. It is, quite frankly, embarrassing – even in the privacy of reading – to witness the stud-strutting tales of men who made love to her or say they did.

The irony, of course, is that for Marilyn Monroe, the F-word was Family. From what she told confidants during these early years, at least, fancy fornication was not a priority. Her satisfaction from men came from turning them on and becoming part of their lives.

'Marilyn Monroe, who was blonde and beautiful and had a sweet little rinky-dink of a voice and all the cleanliness of all the clean American backyards. She was our angel.'

Norman Mailer

'There was no sexual feeling emanating from her. I am sure that was something she put on for the camera.'

Brad Darrach

'The most unsatisfactory men are those who pride themselves on their virility and regard sex as if it were some form of athletics at which you win cups . . . the real lover is the man who can thrill you just by touching your head or smiling into your eyes or by just staring into space,' she said.

Looking at her, what man would have believed her desire for tender pats on the head and quiet times of shared intimacy? Surely, this blonde, moist voluptuary bursting her seams and tumbling out of her bodice was asking to be crushed in a wild embrace. The contradiction between come-hither and make-nice bewildered the men who thought they had a wild tigress by the tail and found instead an affectionate kitten.

The contradiction of Marilyn is evident in a broader sense. For most performers, their personal life is reality away from the spotlight; their roles on screen (or stage) the fantasy they create. For Marilyn, I believe the reverse is true. On screen, the cameras connected with the 'real' woman. From the very start, however small the part, her portrayal is fully realized. She became the waitress in the juke joint luncheonette. She danced and sang her heart out as the burlesque queen's daughter. When she told Groucho Marx a man was following her, her grin directly at the camera made clear that her exaggerated hip-swinging walk was all in good fun and not to be taken seriously.

A Lover and a Mentor

The camera's eye always sees her clearly. Yet in her 'real' life, it's hard to get a clear POV of her. For example, in her relationship with Johnny Hyde. He was the man who did the most for her personal development and for her career, and who arguably loved her the most selflessly of anyone in her entire life. He was her agent and mentor. He launched her movie career. He was in love with her and divorced his wife to marry her. I've seen fuzzy pictures of him and read descriptions of a short, slim, impeccable man who would sit poolside fully clothed while others frolicked in the sunshine.

The factual record is clear enough but it's difficult to 'see' Johnny Hyde and to visualize what he and Marilyn were like as a couple — what they talked about, how they treated with each other. So far as I can tell, there are no extant letters or memos written by Hyde or interviews with him regarding her. He died in December 1950 and remains a shadowy figure. He is described respectfully and with kindness by many including Marilyn herself, grudgingly by others seeking to belittle the affair.

Elia Kazan tells us that Hyde 'prided himself above all on the girls he'd had and subtly let everyone know about his famous successes. His small penis was a symbol of his anxiety, and his whole life was spent laying that anxiety to rest. Marilyn on his arm at Chasen's or Romanoff's did that.'

Johnny Hyde, at fifty-three, and old enough to be her father, was a top Hollywood agent when he and Marilyn met in Palms Springs in 1949. His clients included Rita Hayworth, Esther Williams, Al Jolson, Bob Hope and Lana Turner. He was that rarity in Lotus Land, a gentleman, well-read and courteous to women in an industry that treated starlets like meat on the hoof.

He became her Henry Higgins, she his willing Eliza Doolittle. Terminally ill with heart disease, he may have had the precognition of the dying. He 'saw' the talent inside the surface beauty and the emotional range his efforts would allow her to express. Under his tutelage, she played two dazzling roles in a matter of months, each totally different from the other. In *The Asphalt Jungle*, she was the darkly troubling erotic innocent, in *All About Eve*, the 'dumb blonde' who was nobody's fool.

Hyde became stage 'mother', psychiatrist and lover. Cynics like Kazan have speculated on his physical ability to perform sexually as if that were the sole criterion of love. As Marilyn herself said, 'He was a gentle, kind, brilliant man and I had never known anyone like him. It was Johnny who inspired me to read good books and enjoy good music.' Hyde Pygmalioned her appearance, arranged for plastic surgery on her chin, refined the brassy blondeness of her hair, chose her wardrobe and then, in true Professor Higgins style, introduced her into the upper echelons of Hollywood royalty. Moguls might dismiss her as another blonde — Harry Cohn, who was known for his pungent vocabulary, called her a pig. Yet Johnny Hyde quietly persisted until he prevailed.

'You're going to be a great movie star.'

Johnny Hyde to Marilyn Monroe

The conceit that talent will always find recognition, that cream rises to the top is not necessarily so. There is no Hall of Failure for those who miss the boat. By the time Marilyn met Johnny Hyde, she had been dropped by both 20th Century-Fox and Columbia Pictures. By now, she was twenty-three, a little long in the tooth for the cheesecake cum starlet cum pin-up routine. If someone didn't take her seriously and soon, she might easily have become one of the vast army of Hollywood rejects, one of the perpetual hopefuls. Life could easily have imitated art, with Marilyn reduced to being the waitress or stripper of her first films with a scrapbook of publicity photos and yellowing press clips in the trunk of her second-hand car 'just in case' she met some producer who might think her 'right' for a part.

Fortunately, Johnny Hyde thought she was 'right' for the role of Angela Phinlay in his good friend John Huston's film *The Asphalt Jungle*. As Huston recalled decades later, '. . . little Johnny Hyde of the William Morris Agency called and said he had a girl just right for the part of Angela — might she read for me?' When Hyde brought her to see him, Huston recognized her from an earlier meeting the year before when some un-named heavy at Columbia wanted Huston to give her a fake screen test as a means of seduction. 'Something about Marilyn elicited my protectiveness,' Huston recalled, declining to go along with the deception.

Huston's test scene for *The Asphalt Jungle* called for Angela to be stretched out on a divan; there was no divan in Huston's office so Marilyn kicked off her shoes, lay down on the floor and auditioned from there. 'I later discovered that Johnny Hyde was in love with her. Johnny was a very fine, very reliable agent and we were friends. But Marilyn didn't get the part because of Johnny. She got it because she was damned good.'

Seeing *The Asphalt Jungle* today is a spooky experience. Marilyn was twenty-three but her Angela conveys the child-whore who simpers 'uncle' at the corrupt sensualist of Louis Calhern. What's spooky is not just the parallel to her real-life relationship with Hyde, it is the terrifying cunning with which Angela manipulates her protector. The scenes between the two of them are primarily in private. There's no need to maintain the uncle-niece fiction, yet Marilyn/Angela clings to the conceit like a life preserver, telling him in the manner of an excited adolescent about the swimsuit she bought and how everyone's going to look at her when she wears it.

When, for reasons of plot, Calhern suggests he send her away on a little trip, she trills excitedly and runs down the hallway, again like a fourteen year old, to get the travel folders she's been saving for just such a possibility. What's so harrowing is the authenticity she draws from her own experience. Marilyn/Angela chooses to ignore the sexual debasement of her situation. One can only infer what acts of devotion the uncle expects of his niece. Instead, she chooses to enjoy being the niece in much the way abused youngsters pretend incest doesn't exist and that they are really 'good little girls'.

The dramatic power of her performance is evident, reviewers applauded her, movie goers wrote Who's-the-blonde? fan mail, yet the powers that were still weren't too impressed. Johnny Hyde now

'She is a beautiful child. I don't think she's an actress at all, not in any traditional sense.'

Constance Collier

knew his days were numbered. His final act of devotion was to get her the Miss Caswell role in the Joe Mankiewicz production, *All About Eve.* Seeing this film now, it's hard to realize it was made just a few months after *The Asphalt Jungle.* For film historians to pass the early Marilyn off as just another blonde who would come into her own later is delightfully disproved by Miss Caswell.

In delicious contrast to the psychological retard of Angela, Miss Caswell is a savvy realist who knows what she has and how she must use it to get ahead. Although she is the 'protegée' of another older man – George Sanders as drama critic Addison DeWitt – the relationship is witty and sophisticated. He introduces her as a graduate of the Copacabana School of Dramatic Art and amiably passes her along to an important producer, instructing her to do herself some good. To which Marilyn sighs, 'Why do they always look like unhappy rabbits?'

By the time Johnny Hyde died in December 1950, he had negotiated a seven-year contract with Fox. Marilyn was with him in Palm Springs when he suffered his final heart attack and followed the ambulance that took him back to Los Angeles and the Cedars of Lebanon hospital. Although he had divorced his wife and his dying whisper had been, 'Be sure Marilyn is treated as one of the family', family lawyers ordered her to get out of the house they had shared and warned her to stay away from the funeral.

According to Marilyn biographer Fred Guiles, Hyde's son, Jimmy, never forgot what happened next. Marilyn attended the funeral anyway, 'screaming my father's name over and over again'.

Elia Kazan's 1987 recollections reflect pride and prejudice. Describing his own insecurities over his slight stature, he is – nearly forty years after the event – equally obsessed with Johnny Hyde's diminutive height, five feet five inches. His memory of Hyde's death and its immediate aftermath differs dramatically from others'. According to Kazan, Marilyn was at 'little Johnny's' side when he died, but the body was whisked away before she could say goodbye.

Learning that he was lying in state at the house, she used her keys to enter the place late at night. 'Whoever was guarding the corpse had gone to bed; the candles had burned low. Marilyn told me she climbed on Johnny and lay on him. In still, silent love she stayed there until she heard the first stirring of the family members in the morning. Then she slipped out of the house – alone in the world.'

Kazan also takes pride in having had an affair with Marilyn a short time later. She was violent in love, he says. 'She had a bomb inside her. Ignite her and she exploded.' When his friend, the Pulitzer Prize-winner Arthur Miller, arrived in Los Angeles for script conferences, Kazan, in an effusion of macho camaraderie, passed Marilyn over to him.

This was 1951, of course, a good five years before Miller divorced his first wife to marry her. Miller has described her instant sexual impact on him and others. Wandering through a Los Angeles bookstore with her, he saw a man staring at her and masturbating, adding, ' . . . the air around her was charged. She had said she liked poetry, and we found some Frost and Whitman and e. e. cummings.'

Clearly frightened by her, he remembers, 'The sight of her was something like pain and I knew I must flee or walk into a doom beyond knowing. With all her radiance she was surrounded by a darkness that perplexed me . . . I had to escape her childish voracity, something like my own unruly appetite for self-gratification.' Back home in Brooklyn, he was torn 'between congratulating myself on having escaped destruction and wondering why I had left.'

Dr Gurdin's Crescent Moon

By 1949, Norma Jean had been Marilyn Monroe for three years, but Marilyn had not yet achieved film stardom. That's when her agent and mentor Johnny Hyde brought her to the surgery of Dr Michael M. Gurdin, the Beverly Hills plastic surgeon. The dynamic and flamboyant Gurdin was often mistaken for Douglas Fairbanks, Jr., and enjoyed a highly respected standing in the film colony. A celebrity's celebrity, he was one of the medical pioneers who raised cosmetic procedures to an art form of physical sculpture.

Gurdin remembers Marilyn and her relationship with Hyde: 'Johnny Hyde loved her and believed in her abilities. She was extremely shy which only added to her incredible personal appeal. She had a country-girl type of beauty, magnificent peaches-and-cream skin and, as we talked, she exuded a compelling sexuality.'

He hastens to assure me that this was his response: 'She was very serious. She didn't flirt as a means of communication the way many young women did – and still do.'

Discussing her career with him, she worried about her ability to act and seemed genuinely embarrassed when Johnny predicted big things for her. Yet, Gurdin recalls, despite her diffidence, she could look at herself dispassionately. 'It wasn't vanity. It was the perfectionism that later drove her to learn to sing and dance like a pro.'

As Johnny Hyde was well aware, the big screen magnified every imperfection. Cameras loved her. She photographed well, he thought – except for one tiny flaw.

'Her chin was a little too flat. In person, you wouldn't notice it, of course!' To the surgeon's practised eye, however, it was obvious. And easy to remedy.

To round out the flatness, he placed a small implant in her chin. Made of solid acrylic, it was about an inch wide and a quarter-inch high, and was shaped like a crescent moon.

'She insisted on seeing it, touching it to see how it felt. She was very interested in the process. She wasn't the least bit squeamish. On the contrary she was very calm and relaxed.'

The procedure took about forty-five minutes and consisted of making an incision inside the mouth between the gum and the lower lip. A 'pocket' was formed against the chin, into which was placed the crescent moon implant. Sutures held the implant firmly in place until the 'pocket' healed. Because the operation only called for a light sedative and local anaesthetic, Johnny Hyde was able to take her home the same day.

As was his post-operative custom, Gurdin checked out her progress several times during the next month and was pleased with the result. So were Marilyn and Johnny – so much so that over the ensuing years, Marilyn referred many film-industry friends to him, and patient and doctor remained friends until her death.

Regarding the rumours of other cosmetic surgery, Dr Gurdin doubts there was any. Apart from the chin, he did not perform any additional procedures. Once, when he asked her if the rumours were true, she denied them vehemently. The last time he saw her was in the summer of 1962, a month before she died.

'By that time, her emotional problems had overtaken her. She had fallen down and hit her face. She had a black eye and was terrified that she had broken her nose.'

Dr Gurdin's examination put that fear to rest. The nose was bruised but not broken. 'Her face would heal; her psyche would not.'

'On the surface, she was still a happy girl. But those who criticized her never saw her like I did, crying like a baby because she often felt herself so inadequate.'

Billy Travilla

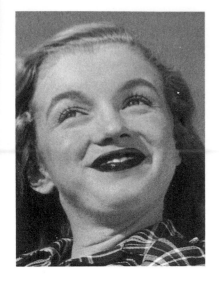

'There'll never be anyone like her for looks, for attitude, for all of it.'

Betty Grable

In retrospect, the still dashing eighty-year-old physician remembers his patient with tenderness and an abiding pride. His crescent moon implant became so much a part of her that she forgot she had it. It helped her to endure her early insecurities and gave her confidence.

'I wish I could have done more for her,' says Gurdin. 'I don't think anyone could have done enough.'

Remembering, too, how devastated he felt on that August day when he learned of her death, he is philosophical about the realities of an entertainment industry that worships youth. 'At least she was spared the indignities of age.'

Neither Love Nor Money...

Elia Kazan was among many on the scene at the time who may have wondered why Marilyn turned down Johnny Hyde's marriage proposal. Many a young actress married movieland movers and shakers – Norma Shearer (to Irving Thalberg), Jean Harlow (to Paul Bern), Jennifer Jones (to David O. Selznick). As Mrs Johnny Hyde, Marilyn could have moved into the Hollywood establishment through the front door and inherited his wealth at his death.

Some may have thought it immoral to be his girl; she thought it immoral to marry a man she didn't love. Romantic, perhaps, but more than that is the proof of her own very personal set of priorities. Wealth was not high on her list. Never, in any of her relationships, including serious love affairs and marriages, did she come close to getting rich. Nor for that matter was she well paid for her film roles. In fact, the only home she ever owned was the modest Brentwood house in which she died.

When she later married Joe DiMaggio and later still Arthur Miller, she was in love . . . or thought she was in love. During the Johnny Hyde period, she was also in love but not with him. The man she most passionately wanted to marry then and for a long torch-carrying time to come, was the slim, handsome music director of Columbia Pictures, Fred Karger.

He would have been perfect for her in every way. When Columbia signed her in 1948, Karger's assignment was to teach her to refine and project her untrained singing voice. Contrary to rumours of dubbing, it is Marilyn herself making her singing debut in *Ladies of the Chorus* and going on to bigger things in *Gentlemen Prefer Blondes*, *Some Like it Hot* and as the touching Cherie doing 'That Old Black Magic' in *Bus Stop*.

While Karger was teaching her – symbolically – 'Every Baby Needs a Da Da Daddy' and 'Anyone Can See I Love You' – he became her main man. He sent her to the orthodontist to have her front teeth straightened. He took her to concerts at the Hollywood Bowl. Most important to her, he took her home to meet his mother and the rest of the large, affectionate Karger family. The family took her to its collective bosom, including his mother Anne – who recognized Marilyn's shyness – and Karger's two children by a previous marriage whose fondest memories are of the hours she spent playing games with them on the floor.

Anne Karger encouraged her son to marry Marilyn and, failing that, maintained her friendship with her almost-daughter until Marilyn's death. In the marriage-go-round of Hollywood, Karger later married actor Ronald Reagan's first wife, Jane Wyman, who won an Oscar for *Johnny Belinda* and TV fame as the matriarch of 'Falcon Crest'. Karger, an accomplished composer, wrote the theme for

From Here to Eternity and died of leukaemia on 5 August 1979, seventeen years to the day after Marilyn's death.

The critics creamed *Ladies of the Chorus* but at least one, Tibor Krekes of the *Motion Picture Herald*, said, 'One of the brightest spots is Miss Monroe's singing.'

Lost love is the core of tragedy. With Karger, she may have had a chance. With him, she would have had a brilliant and skilled professional coach to improve her performance, an affectionate husband and lover she was nuts about, and a warm and supportive extended family. She would most likely have had the children she so wistfully desired and a solid foundation to her life instead of the rootless search for happiness that always wound up in a dead end.

As Karger's wife, the studio bosses may have taken her more seriously as an actress and comedian rather than the chuckle-headed bimbo. Tony Curtis said she kissed like Hitler. Dore Schary, head of MGM, dismissed her performance in *The Asphalt Jungle* as 'limited' and dropped her option. To them, a sexy blonde with a saucy walk was only that, interchangeable with other sexy blondes.

Conjecture is a what-if parlour game at best. Still, with Karger's guidance, she may have had a chance of attaining the role she so desperately wanted, Grushenka in *The Brothers Karamazov*. The industry reared back on its collective dignity and roared at her effrontery. General ignorance of Dostoevsky doubtless contributed to the sneering merriment. Anyone who'd read the novel would have at least conceded her suitability for the pivotal role of the elder Karamazov's mistress and the torment she incites in his son, Dimitri, which destroys them both.

Maria Schell's eventual portrayal, though largely ignored, was never ridiculed. Marilyn's humiliation extended through skits and jokes about her being in bed with the Brothers Karamazov and imitations of her whispery inability to so much as pronounce *Kaza-maz-araz-arov*. It's no wonder she left for New York where people at least pretended to be interested in her mind.

Fred Karger's mother was not the only woman to be deeply touched by Marilyn and to feel protective towards her. Emmeline Snively was her first 'professional mother'. As head of the Blue Book agency, Mrs Snively enrolled her in a modelling course to correct the neophyte's posture and grooming, and deferred payment until the youngster could be sent out on assignments.

Her biggest contribution was changing Norma Jean's smile, and she tried, unsuccessfully, to modify the 'horrible' walk, revealing years later, 'that wiggle wasn't good for fashion models but we couldn't change it. I'm glad now, of course.'

People made fun of Marilyn. She was an easy target. Ridicule, rather than imitation, is the sincerest form of flattery. But it is more hurtful to the target. There is small comfort in knowing that people make sport of what they envy, fear or don't understand. Marilyn seemed to court it and pretend it didn't bother her. The latter is hard to accept. Ridicule is a raging cancer of our society. Making fun of people ain't funny. It's human vandalism, a form of violence that diminishes the bully as much as the victim.

Taking potshots at Marilyn was a spectator sport from the start. They made fun of her books as well as her looks. For the uneducated, words and ideas promise a paradise of riches. She bought books the way some women buy shoes — stacks of them. Emerson, Joyce, Thomas Wolfe, Rilke, Whitman, Chekhov, Tolstoy, Dostoevsky, biographies of Lincoln, Shakespeare's plays and sonnets. One of her earliest purchases was *De Humani Corporis Fabrica*, a study of human anatomy by the sixteenth century scholar, Andreas Vesalius. She used it to learn about bone structure and worked out with weights long before the fitness craze.

'She had this absolute unerring touch with comedy ... she acted as if she didn't quite understand why it was funny. Which is what made it so funny.'

George Cukor

Wherever she lived, there were pictures from magazines on the walls: Eleanora Duse, Albert Einstein and her idol, Lincoln, as well as prints of Matisse, Cézanne, Dürer, Fra Angelica and da Vinci. Who was she kidding? How pretentious! There's no way of knowing if she actually read the books. The point is she knew what she didn't know. Gathering books to her bosom was a first step. All intellectual pursuit begins as pretension, the show-off spouting Proust or reciting Ovid. The scholar translating Homer. The 'interpreters' telling everyone what everyone from Chaucer to Thackeray to Kahlil Gibran really mean. There's no way of knowing if she discovered Walter Pater: '*To burn always with this hard, gemlike flame, to maintain this ecstasy, is success in life.*'

Her walk was something else, a kind of Mae West put-on for the fans. A more appropriate target for jokes, it was good-natured by design and elicited good-natured if sometimes over-heated reactions. *Life* magazine photographer Phillipe Halsman said, '. . . with every step, her derrière seemed to wink at the onlooker.' He found it incredible that in those early days '20th Century-Fox never thought of shooting her from behind.' Critic Pauline Kael said, 'She would bat her Bambi eyelashes, lick her messy, suggestive open mouth, wiggle that pert and tempting bottom and use her hushed voice to caress us with dizzying innuendos.' Hollywood journalist James Bacon said, 'Her derrière looked like two puppies fighting under a silk sheet.'

German actress Hildegard Neff described Marilyn at an awards dinner wearing a red dress that was too tight, her eyes half closed, mouth half open. The audience sniggers as she trips to the microphone. 'The walk is absurd . . . they stare at the dress, wait for it to burst and liberate the bosom, the belly, the bottom.'

Neff was touched by Marilyn's need for attention. Not so Joan Crawford. As Hollywood's reigning *grande dame,* Crawford met the starlet at Joe Schenck's house and loftily invited her for tea and some advice on how to dress. Some time later, when Marilyn was sewn into the scandalous gold lamé gown for the *Photoplay* Awards, and stole the spotlight, La Crawford had a fit. 'It was like a burlesque show,' she told columnist Bob Thomas. 'Sex plays a tremendously important part in every person's life . . . She [Marilyn] should be told the public likes provocative feminine personalities, but it also likes to know that underneath it all, the actresses are ladies.'

'She was a very healthy girl when she came on the scene, physically and mentally ... people picked on her, she was terribly abused for no reason. She became sick — and posthumously they gave her acclaim.'

Ann-Margret

Every Girl Needs Her Mother

Many months before the 'birth' of Marilyn Monroe, Mrs Snively changed her professional name to Jean Norman and got her assignments that put her on covers of magazines like *Laff, Peek, See* and *US Camera.* When a Howard Hughes assistant phoned to offer an RKO screen test, Emmeline did what only a selfless, caring mother would do. Not wanting to ruin the girl's chances and feeling inexperienced in making film deals, she turned things over to another woman, Helen Ainsworth of the National Concert Artists Corporation, who in turn told Ben Lyon at Fox that Howard Hughes was after her client.

Unlike most of the others Norma Jean left behind when she became Marilyn, Emmeline Snively remained a dear and honoured friend. A decade later, when her protégée had achieved international stardom, the older woman was personally invited by Marilyn to the set of *There's No Business Like Show Business.* In a way, it was like the proud mother seeing her child perform in a school play.

The next surrogate mother was Natasha Lytess. Head drama coach at Columbia Pictures, she was a refugee from Nazi Germany where she had studied with the famous Max Reinhardt. Natasha fell on Marilyn like a sculptor with a lump of virgin clay. She introduced her to the life of the European intellectual, and was the first to make her think about emotional motivation for her development of acting technique and for her on-camera performance.

A lonely widow, Lytess made Marilyn the centre of her life. Herself an actress in her youth, she poured her energies into Marilyn's career, appearing on the set with her during filming and causing chaos when Marilyn looked to her for approval after each take. Fortunately for Marilyn, she sought refuge with Natasha when Johnny Hyde died. A few days after the funeral Natasha found a note from Marilyn reading, 'I leave my car and fur stole to Natasha!' She had swallowed a bottle of sleeping pills. Natasha nursed her back to health. A few months later, when Natasha needed a throat operation, Marilyn sold her mink coat to pay for it.

'Marilyn needed me like a dead man needs a coffin.'

Natasha Lytess

Rumours persist of a lesbian relationship between the two women. Natasha's possessiveness was overwhelming, Marilyn's need for her devotion and advice was equally so. That for a time Marilyn submitted totally to Natasha's control suggests an intimate dependency that might have been sexual as well. Whatever the physical specifics, Natasha was ultimately replaced by other nurturing mother figures including Amy Greene, the wife of Marilyn's business partner, photographer Milton Greene, and Paula Strasberg, the wife of Actors' Studio founder Lee Strasberg.

Marilyn was to live with the Greenes in Connecticut while preparing to marry Arthur Miller and go to England to co-star with Laurence Olivier in *The Prince and the Showgirl*. Footage of an Edward R. Murrow TV visit shows a demure Marilyn in the filial protective custody of her new 'family'. Lee and Paula Strasberg and their daughter Susan also opened their family home to the needy orphan and welcomed her to the extended family of 'sisters and brothers' in the Strasberg classes.

From early on, her longing to *belong* added a touching dimension to many of her roles. As early as *Clash by Night*, when she played Peggy, a worker in a California fish cannery in love with Barbara Stanwyck's brother Joe, played by Keith Andes. In one scene, Marilyn shows Joe's ring to her future sister-in-law with a mixture of girlish excitement and fear of rejection. When Stanwyck hugs her and welcomes her, Marilyn's joy and relief provide proof of her ability to 'tell' the camera what she could not express to those around her.

Years later, in the final scene of *Bus Stop* she packs the same emotional wallop, only more so, when her cowboy suitor Don Murray puts his sheepskin jacket around her shoulders to protect her from the cold. He stands behind her, her face is to the camera, her eyes suddenly, radiantly conveying her ecstatic bliss at finding true love, personal respect and a real home for the first time.

Posing nude for Tom Kelley caused shock waves when the resultant calendar was distributed. One wonders what the fuss was about. Goya painted his beloved Duchess both clothed and in the all-together. As Marilyn herself said, 'Nobody ever objected to Botticelli's *Venus*.'

Considering what was on the sexual horizon in magazines like *Hustler* and films like *Deep Throat*, it was a sign of those times when the US Post Office banned the sale by mail of cocktail coasters featuring the Marilyn nude, branding it 'obscene, lewd, lascivious and indecent'.

In a candid reflection on nudity, Marilyn said her desire for attention caused problems for her during Sunday church services. 'No sooner was I in the pew with the organ playing and everybody singing a hymn than the impulse would come to me to take off all my clothes. I wanted desperately to stand up naked for God and everyone to see. I had to clench my teeth and sit on my hands to keep myself from undressing.'

She remembered dreaming about it: 'I entered the church wearing a hoop skirt with nothing under it. The people would be lying on their backs in the church aisle and I would step over them, and they would look up at me.'

We can assume the lonely, introverted orphan learned about life and love from the movies. In the morality of Thirties and Forties movies, there were good girls and bad girls. The good girls generally got the man. The bad girls were infinitely more glamorous and generally had a good excuse for being bad. What's more, they knew how to manipulate men into doing what they wanted, often to kill their husbands. Good girls in the movies sighed and cried a lot. Bad girls knew about sex and got lots of hot enjoyment from their evil seductions before the laws of cinema justice caught up with them and they had to die for their sins.

In *The Postman Always Rings Twice*, Lana Turner gets John Garfield to kill her husband and then dies in a car crash. In *Double Indemnity*, Barbara Stanwyck – as a blonde wearing an ankle bracelet and a towel – gets Fred MacMurray to kill her husband and then, in an added twist, tries to kill him and gets herself killed instead.

'When you look at Marilyn on the screen, you don't want anything bad to happen to her. You really care that she should be all right – happy.'

Natalie Wood

The Sailor and His Lady

Some fifteen years after Marilyn Monroe's death, Jim Dougherty told a *People* magazine reporter, 'If I hadn't gone into the Merchant Marines during World War II, she would still be Mrs Dougherty today.'

Maybe, but doubtful. Considering her single-minded determination to 'be somebody', it's hard to believe she would have been content as a housewife and mother. It's important to remember that she was a sixteen-year-old schoolgirl when she married Jim Dougherty in 1942, and that he was the star attraction. A local student leader, football hero and owner of a flashy blue Ford convertible, he was handsome, blue-eyed, a terrific dancer and much sought after by hordes of smitten young women, including a beauty pageant winner.

Norma Jean must surely have felt lucky that with a choice of the prettiest and liveliest girls in the area, he chose to marry her. From all reports, including her own, the first few years of their marriage were a continuing honeymoon – until the war took him to sea and sent her to a war plant. That's where the *if* factor began to accelerate. *If* Jim had not gone to sea and *if* Norma Jean had not gone to work and *if* a photographer had not taken her picture and *if* Emmeline Snively had not seen it in an Army magazine and suggested she become a model and *if* Emmeline had not sent her to Joe Jasgur's studio for test shots and *if* Norma Jean had not shown Joe's photographs to Ben Lyon at 20th Century-Fox – would she be living in contented retirement with ex-policeman Jim Dougherty today?

Maybe. But doubtful. Anything is possible, of course, but Dougherty's own personal recollections of the year she traded in Norma Jean for a new identity as Marilyn Monroe suggest a compelling inevitability in her behaviour. He waited thirty years to tell his side of what happened in 1946 and even at that remove, his pain and bewilderment are evident. In 1976, *The Secret Happiness of Marilyn* was published by Playboy Press. His book seems to have disappeared completely – and has been out of print for years – but a Florida 'Marilyn' collector, Joe Stewart, was kind enough to take a copy of the pages that refer to this period, documenting the sorrow with which Dougherty battled.

Jim blames his absence for her decision to become a model. In realistic terms, she understood why he had to be away and accepted it. Psychologically, however, Dougherty was convinced she felt abandoned — the illegitimate orphan child left in the lurch yet again.

Although the Second World War had ended in August 1945, Dougherty was asked to remain in the Maritime Service for several more months. He returned home on leave regularly that autumn, only to find his wife busy with her modelling classes. Christmas turned out to be a disaster. He was home — but she had accepted a location assignment with a photographer, leaving Jim to have Christmas dinner without her.

'In January, we had a showdown,' he remembers in his memoir. 'I just told her that she would have to choose between a modelling career and maybe the movies or a home life with me like we had in Catalina.'

A few months later, after she filed for divorce, he returned home to try to talk her out of it. 'She was nearly broke. She had sold our silverware and pawned just about everything except the radio.'

It was then that he realized he had lost the fight to keep his marriage together. Norma Jean knew what she wanted. He couldn't offer her anything except promises. His next trip took him across the Pacific to China. It was June 1946, their fourth wedding anniversary. As his ship made its way up the Yangtze River to Shanghai, he was absolutely miserable. 'There was nothing to celebrate.'

Ever hopeful, however, he gathered up a collection of exotic gifts for her — jade rings and bracelets, carved boxes and a large camphor wood chest. Norma Jean had not written to him but she was still uppermost in his thoughts.

Back aboard ship, a letter awaited him. It was from a Nevada divorce lawyer. Now it was official: Norma Jean wanted a divorce. In the months that followed, Jim Dougherty did all he could to delay things, still clinging to the hope that he could change her mind. For starters, he refused to sign the divorce papers until he returned to Los Angeles and they could have a long talk. When they did meet, he expressed his deep concern about her ability to cope on her own in the tough world of show business. He warned her about the tremendous emotional and physical pressures she would have to endure.

Despite the strong sexual attraction they still felt for each other, Norma Jean was adamant. There would be no reconciliation.

'I'm sorry she made the decision she did, sorrier today when I know how it all ended,' wrote Dougherty.

The day he signed the divorce papers and gave them to her personally, she told him about her new name.

'Marilyn Monroe. What do you think of it?' She beamed.

'It's beautiful, just beautiful,' Jim Dougherty assured her. He remembers her reaction to his approval. 'She just lit up, as though my opinion was something she cared about.'

His emotion is evident as he adds wistfully, 'Maybe it was.'

'Our marriage was a good marriage ... I wonder if she's forgotten how much in love we really were.'

Jim Dougherty

'She knows the world, but this know-ledge has not lowered her great and benevolent dignity ... its darkness has not dimmed her goodness.'

Edith Sitwell

The Death of Marilyn

I wept when Marilyn died, deep, convulsive sobs that surprised me with their intensity. It wasn't for the death of a movie star. It was that she died alone and on a Saturday night, date night, party night, the night to be with your nearest and dearest. How could it be? Marilyn Monroe alone on a Saturday night? In summer? when everyone else was at the beach or in the backyard or somewhere having fun? And making love? The thought of her lying naked and dead with the phone off the hook offended the most intelligent woman's romantic vision of the superstar who could presumably snap her fingers and have any man she wanted.

This kind of aloneness is beyond lonely. It is integral to orphanhood. Arthur Miller recalls how Marilyn could walk into a crowded room and 'spot anyone there who had lost parents as a child or had spent time in orphanages ... there is a "Do you like me?" in an orphan's eyes, an appeal out of bottomless loneliness that no parented person can really know.'

Birthdays and holidays like New Year's Eve are like super-Saturday Night. On her twentieth birthday in 1946, she was alone in Nevada, sitting out her divorce from James Dougherty and wondering what the future would bring. On New Year's Eve, 1951, she had – incredibly – no date, no plans, no invitations. According to Hollywood writer James Bacon, she phoned him, saying 'I don't want to stay home alone on New Year's Eve. Can I go to a party with you?' Bacon may have been her lover and friend but he was also married and said his wife would not appreciate it.

More than most women, she had the chance to live out her romantic fantasies. She was fiction-become-fact, the orphan who becomes a movie star and marries not one but two of the most famous and respected men of her generation. She had it all, right? Beauty, talent, sex appeal, intelligence. So what was her problem? Was she simply proof of the old platitude about the worst thing that can happen to a dreamer is for the dream to come true?

Stardom was supposed to mean love and approval, not battles over contracts, ridicule, miscarriages, pills and death at thirty-six. Love was supposed to mean picket-fence contentment, affectionate intimacy and children.

'Togetherness' was the abiding theme of post-war America. The man was the breadwinner, the woman waited for his arrival home with a steaming casserole and a child of each sex clinging to her snowy white apron strings. Marilyn's fantasies seem to have combined this rose-tinted domestic bliss with the romantic dream of the knight on the white charger.

What happened to her really is the extreme of what happened to ordinary women raised on the same romantic expectations. Prince Charming turned out to be unaware of the romantic mantle placed on his shoulders. He was at first bewildered and then exasperated at what 'the little woman' expected of him. Candy, flowers, sweet nothings were for him the tools of seduction, what a man had to go through to get his rocks off or to get a wife. He did not expect the marriage contract to include continuing and ardent attention.

When they met, 'Joltin' Joe DiMaggio was a superstar icon in his own right – rich, famous, worshipped internationally by sports fans. He was also divorced and besieged by eager, adoring women wherever he went. As it turns out, Marilyn was not one of them. Baseball was not of primary interest to her. She only vaguely knew who Joe DiMaggio was.

His interest in meeting her stemmed from a publicity photograph of Marilyn in shorts, tight sweater and spike heels with members of the Chicago White Sox baseball team 'coaching' her on how to hold the bat. DiMaggio saw the photograph in the newspaper, liked what he saw and asked a friend to arrange a blind date.

According to Anthony Summers, author of *Goddess: The Secret Lives of Marilyn Monroe,* Marilyn said, 'I don't care to meet him. I don't like men in loud clothes with checked suits and big muscles and pink ties.' To her surprise and delight, DiMaggio was a lean, greying, confident man given to conservative suits, and twelve years her senior. The courtship was conducted in public. All the world loved these lovers and wanted them to marry and live happily ever after. The only trouble was what each expected of the other.

Joe was the traditional old-fashioned macho Sicilian. He literally wanted to 'take her away from all this' — including her career — and to have her home painting her toenails and patiently awaiting his return while he stayed out carousing with the boys.

He wanted her to give up the sexy clothes that had attracted him in the first place. He didn't want 'his woman' exposed to the lecherous eyes of other men. She was hurt by the coldness that replaced the pre-marital warmth. When push came to shove, she was basically alone. And when *Photoplay* magazine gave her its prestigious 'Fastest Rising Star' award, all of Hollywood was in attendance at the Beverly Hills Hotel. With one exception: her husband, who refused to accompany her.

'She had her problems. She was disturbed in many areas, and those who weren't close friends of hers may not have realized how grave some of her personal problems were.'

Peter Lawford

Arriving on the arm of columnist Sidney Skolsky, she wore a gold lamé gown that she had been sewn into. As she sashayed down the aisle to her seat, host Jerry Lewis jumped up and down on a table, black-tied men in the audience howled and *Playboy* founder Hugh Hefner decided to put her on the cover of his first issue several months later. One can only imagine DiMaggio's reactions to the outrageous gold gown, the *Playboy* cover — and her infamous 'Golden Dreams' nude designating her the magazine's first 'Sweetheart of the Month'.

Playboy made magazine history as the first high-quality publication to combine the best writers in the world — Hemingway and the like — with the best photographs of women in various stages of undress. To Joe, the ultimate humiliation was the famous *Seven Year Itch* billboard, hundreds of feet high over Times Square, showing Marilyn with her white dress billowing up above her waist exposing her panties. He couldn't understand why she did it. She couldn't understand why he was pissed off. A passing comment by a journalist pinpoints the break-up in a single gesture. Marilyn was putting her arms around Joe in an affectionate hug. He pushed her away. End of story.

In divorce court, she said, 'He didn't talk to me. He was cold. He was indifferent to me as a human being and an artist . . . He watched television instead of talking to me.' End of marriage.

Arthur Miller was something else, another species of Prince Charming come to woo the lady fair with books and ideas and a humanity that she, the high-school drop-out, idealized. Like DiMaggio, he too endured the lip-smacking envy and the speculations about his special appeal and their private life. And he, too, resented his role as consort, although the marriage brought him stage centre in her worldwide theatre, a far bigger and more publicly exposed place than his literary milieu.

The Child Inside

I wonder if DiMaggio or Miller ever saw the Jasgur photographs and realized that this awkward, yearning Norma Jean was still quaking inside the glorious goddess Marilyn Monroe had become.

'She has more guts than a slaughter-house. Being with her, people want not to die. She's all woman, the most womanly woman in the world.'

Arthur Miller

Making judgment on another's life is presumptuous at best. To nod wisely some thirty years after Marilyn's death and murmur it's just as well she died when she did on the crest of the wave is a beyond-presumption risk taken for the sole purpose of making a point.

Ridicule had followed her like a dark shadow all her life. Even at her zenith, people made fun of her. There is a distinction between provoking jokes and becoming one. By the summer of 1962, she had reached her prime and would soon begin to show the ravages of illness, pills and fear that were destroying her from the inside out. she could not have tolerated the physical debasement of middle age in her own eyes or in the pitying contempt of the future. Her pleasure and satisfaction in her own nudity would soon be shattered by the inevitable thickening of her flesh and the disfiguring marks of time. I can't imagine her playing *Baby Jane* grotesques like Joan Crawford and Bette Davis, or haughty matriarchs like Jane Wyman. Like Joan Collins, she had the looks to age spectacularly into her fifties but unlike Alexis, the killer shark we hated to love, Marilyn could never have been a woman of the world in a world that was rapidly changing ... especially for women.

In her last weeks of life, she never looked more exquisitely, ethereally beautiful — almost other-worldly, as if the transition from life had subtly begun. The contours of her face were delicately honed, her body slim and lean in a last-stand contradiction of nature. She had been softly rounded and voluptuous when she posed for Joseph Jasgur in 1946, and rosy as a Fragonard two years later, a womanly girl, in the infamous nude-on-red-velvet session with Tom Kelley. Photographs of her in 1962 were shot in colour but she is shades of pale, her skin like ivory satin, as if her life blood were slowly drying up, leaving behind an eggshell façade doomed to crack.

Like many women, I feel a strange, abiding connection to Marilyn. She epitomizes the law of polarity. Her exterior 'Marilyn' and interior 'Norma Jean' are opposite extremes of the same energy. She was an enigma, always at war with herself and unable to achieve completion.

Off-camera she was the Marilyn she created, brazen, provocative, quixotic, single-minded in her obsession with herself. On camera, Norma Jean came through with all her naked yearnings and uncertainties, and with the whispery 'baby' voice of the neglected child.

As Norma Jean she put on an act and then became the act and got stuck with it. People wanted Marilyn. They could deal with the sexy, hip-swinging Marilyn. Norma Jean was a turn-off. Joe DiMaggio wanted Marilyn the movie star as a trophy to show his friends, not the complex Norma Jean who needed cuddling and reassurance. Arthur Miller wanted Marilyn in much the same way as Johnny Hyde, as raw material to mould, in Miller's case intellectually. By then, the imprisoned Norma Jean was disintegrating from pills and booze and psychic wounds and was past rescue by the most patient, intuitive husband.

Every woman experiences her polarity to a degree. We each of us create a 'Marilyn' exterior of our own design, a persona we hope will attract love, friends, attention and respect for our talents, ideas and ambitions. We all of us are actresses starring in our own scenarios, jockeying for position and praise. We are prepared to give autographs. Meanwhile, the interior Norma Jean in each of us is whimpering with insecurity, a sodden mess of doubt and despair, a worn tape deck repeating the endless refrain, *Why doesn't anyone understand? ... Why is everyone so mean to me? ... Can't they see how helpless I am, how hurt, how deprived, how tired, how frightened, how lonely, how ...*

Poet and playwright Norman Rosten encouraged Marilyn's interest in writing. 'She liked poetry. It was a shortcut for her. She understood with the instinct of a poet, that it led directly into the heart of experience.' Among the poems she wrote is this:

Life — I am both of your directions
Somehow remaining
Hanging downward the most
Strong as a cobweb in the wind.

Her cobweb is still around, stronger than ever, brushing gently against our collective face.

'In a way we are all guilty. We built her to the skies. We loved her but left her lonely and afraid when she needed us most.'

Hedda Hopper

Remembering Marilyn...

'Marilyn is quite a product of our generation and it would be an honour for any girl to be able to emulate her' **Joanne Woodward.** 'I miss her. It was like going to the dentist, making a picture with her. It was hell at the time, but after it was over, it was wonderful' **Earl Wilson.** 'It was Hollywood that destroyed her – she was the victim of her friends' **Joe DiMaggio.** '... A star is only good as a star. You don't fit into anything less. Yes, it's there. I can feel it. I see a hundred actresses a week ... they haven't got what you have' **Johnny Hyde to Marilyn Monroe.** 'Still she hangs like a bat in the heads of men who have met her, and none of us will ever forget her' **Sammy Davis, Jr.** 'Miss Monroe is one of the greatest comedy actresses of our time. She is simply superb' **Vladimir Nabokov.** 'Marilyn had a childlike quality which made men adore her. Yet women weren't jealous' **Ben Lyon.** 'She will go on eternally' **Jacqueline Kennedy Onassis.** 'She was a fool to kill herself ... she could have been the first great woman director because she understood how to make movies' **Andy Warhol.** 'There may be an exact psychiatric term for what was wrong with her. I don't know ... I think she was quite mad. The mother was mad and poor Marilyn was mad' **George Cukor.** '... I couldn't dislike Marilyn. She had no meanness in her – no bitchery. She just had to concentrate on herself and the people who were there only for her' **Lauren Bacall.** 'She was ten feet under water... a wall of thick cotton ... you stick a pin in her and eight days later it says "ouch"' **Nunnally Johnson.** 'I think she's going to be one of the most popular actresses the movies have ever known' **Sidney Skolsky, 1962.** 'She was a cunning, ambitious woman who exploited people and situations ... She used others at least as often as she herself was used' **Tony Sciacca.** 'She looked a fright at first, but my, how she worked!' **Emmeline Snively.** 'She usually draped herself in a towel. If it slid off, OK. She didn't care if she had anything on or not and this was before nudity was in. She was ahead of her time' **George Masters.** 'I was as good as could be, and, Marilyn! Marilyn was quite wonderful, the best of all. What do you know?' **Sir Laurence Olivier.** 'Directing her was like directing Lassie. You need fourteen takes to get each one of them right' **Otto Preminger.** 'She is more nervous than any other actress I have ever known. But nervousness for an actress is not a handicap. It is a sign of sensitivity' **Lee Strasberg.** 'I thought, surely she won't come over, she's so small scale, but when I saw her on the stage, my goodness, how it came over' **Dame Sybil Thorndike.** 'I took her as a serious actress before I ever met her ... I think she might turn into the greatest tragic actress that can be imagined' **Arthur Miller.** 'She was the type who would join in and wash up the supper dishes even if you didn't ask her' **Carl Sandburg.** 'She's frightened to death of the public who think she is so sexy. My God, if they only knew' **Whitey Snyder.** '...The complete transformation, like Dr Jekyll and Mr Hyde, her mannerisms, her gestures, everything was changed, not only her dress and make-up ...She was phenomenal to watch' **George Masters.** '...As you get to know her, you find out she's no goddamn gold-plated birdbrain. She's a serious dame' **Cameron Mitchell.** 'Marilyn would have been sixty this year. If the feminist movement had existed, it might have saved her life' **Gloria Steinem, 1986.** 'She liked to shock – she could look both magnificent or hideous – like a dirty little bum or a sex queen...' **Billy Travilla.** 'Can Marilyn ever be happy?' **Hedda Hopper.** 'In death, as in life, the woman who was Marilyn Monroe continues to exert a power I've never been able to fully understand or explain' **Ted Jordan.**

'I used to think as I looked out on the Hollywood night — there must be thousands of girls sitting alone like me, dreaming of becoming a movie star. But I'm not going to worry about them. I'm dreaming the hardest.'

Marilyn Monroe

Emmeline Snively of the Blue Book Model Agency asked Hollywood photographer Joe Jasgur to take some test shots of one of her newcomers, Norma Jean Dougherty. He photographed her in a small street behind Beverly Boulevard in West Hollywood, 'stealing' an hour from his schedule to do it. Then, in his darkroom, Norma Jean watched the developing and printing. 'Magic,' she whispered, when her face slowly began to materialize on a blank sheet of paper. '*Magic!*'

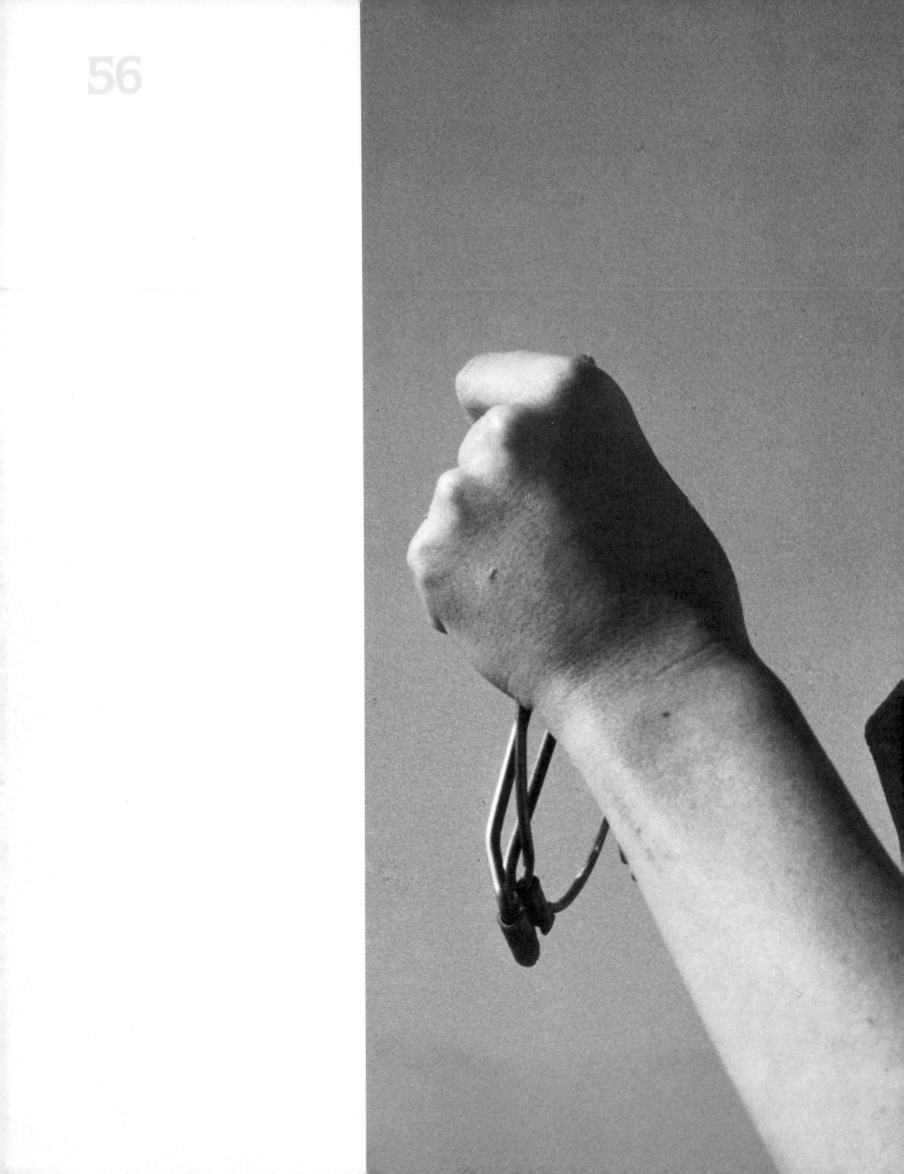

Jasgur frequently chose Zuma Beach for shooting pin-up features. He took Norma Jean there for shoots on 18 and 23 March 1946, and to add to the fun on the 23rd he invited the cast of a local production of a time-worn melodrama, *The Drunkards*.

In the months following the March shoots, Joe Jasgur photographed Norma Jean several times with other young members of Emmeline Snively's Blue Book Model Agency, shooting her in the pin-up conventions of the day — as a *fräulein*, a milk maid, a bathing beauty.

'It might be kind of a relief to be finished.'

Marilyn Monroe

MODEL RELEASE

City _Hollywood_

For value received, I hereby consent th

Jos. Gregor

attached, may be used or sold by Joseph J

ration, advertising or publication in any m

covenant that I am over twenty-one years

Thom

Mary

_____
WITNESS

outdoor beach pho